W9-CAW-140

MAINE MEMORIES

MAINE MEMORIES

ELIZABETH COATSWORTH

THE STEPHEN GREENE PRESS

BRATTLEBORO, VERMONT 1968

The author and publisher are grateful to Crowell, Collier and Macmillan, Inc., for permission to use material from *Country Neighborhood* and *Maine Ways.*

The illustrative map on page x is by Grevis Melville

 Designed by R. L. Dothard Associates. Printed and bound in the United States of America by The Book Press Incorporated, Brattleboro, Vermont.
Library of Congress catalog card number: 68–18586

Contents

Contents

Prologue

READING OVER these chapters, I am filled with a nostalgia for those years of our early middle age, when our two daughters were growing up, in a simpler world, and our garden was plowed each year by oxen. In those days our neighbors on this back road still farmed their land, and the serene hours were filled with work and pleasure.

We must have had worries and frustrations, but if so, I have forgotten them. What writing we both did in those mornings at our desks! What picnics we had at noon by ourselves, or sometimes with other families! What explorations we went on by canoe and on foot along old wood-trails, or by snowshoe across the frozen lake, or by car, following nameless roads! There were long visits with our neighbors, and more formal parties, now and then. At all times a book was tucked beside the casserole in the noonday picnic basket and Henry read aloud after we had eaten, perhaps at our own fresh-water cove before we went swimming, perhaps under the pines, or on headlands looking over the sea towards Monhegan Island. In the evenings he most often read Shakespeare, while I darned socks and my mother hemmed tea napkins.

Our world has changed. We have eight young grandchildren, four of whom are just back with their parents from two years in Athens. Our other daughter lives with her family in California, and often comes East in the summer, bringing a child or two to spend a few weeks with us or near us. Although we still go driving, most of our hours are spent on the sun porch in the shelter of the ell, with its view of the lake and its many, many birds. We entice raccoons and skunks for late-afternoon handouts and they and their children often eat at the same time as we do, with only the many-paned big window between us. All summer we have a ballet of eight chipmunks which, with snow, changes to a dance of squirrels.

Now the house has central heating and electricity. It is warm and cheerful, filled with plants, in the parlor an old marjoram bush, and a six-foot geranium tree which seems to be always in bloom, and in my bedroom there is a large orange tree, besides lesser plants. But we have kept all our old wood stoves for use on particularly cold days, and emergency oil lamps still stand on their brackets in kitchen and pantry. Of course there are many books, and, better still, friends drop in to see us, especially in summer when half the world comes to Maine.

In combining chapters from two earlier books I have made certain changes—what writer can resist the need to do some re-writing? And I have added several chapters based on the notebooks I kept after writing *Maine Ways,* so that the new material covers about the same decade between the mid-1930's and the end of the Second World War.

Reading this book now, it is the story of a lost world, lost to us, at all events.

Chimney Farm
Nobleboro, Maine
January 1968

ELIZABETH COATSWORTH

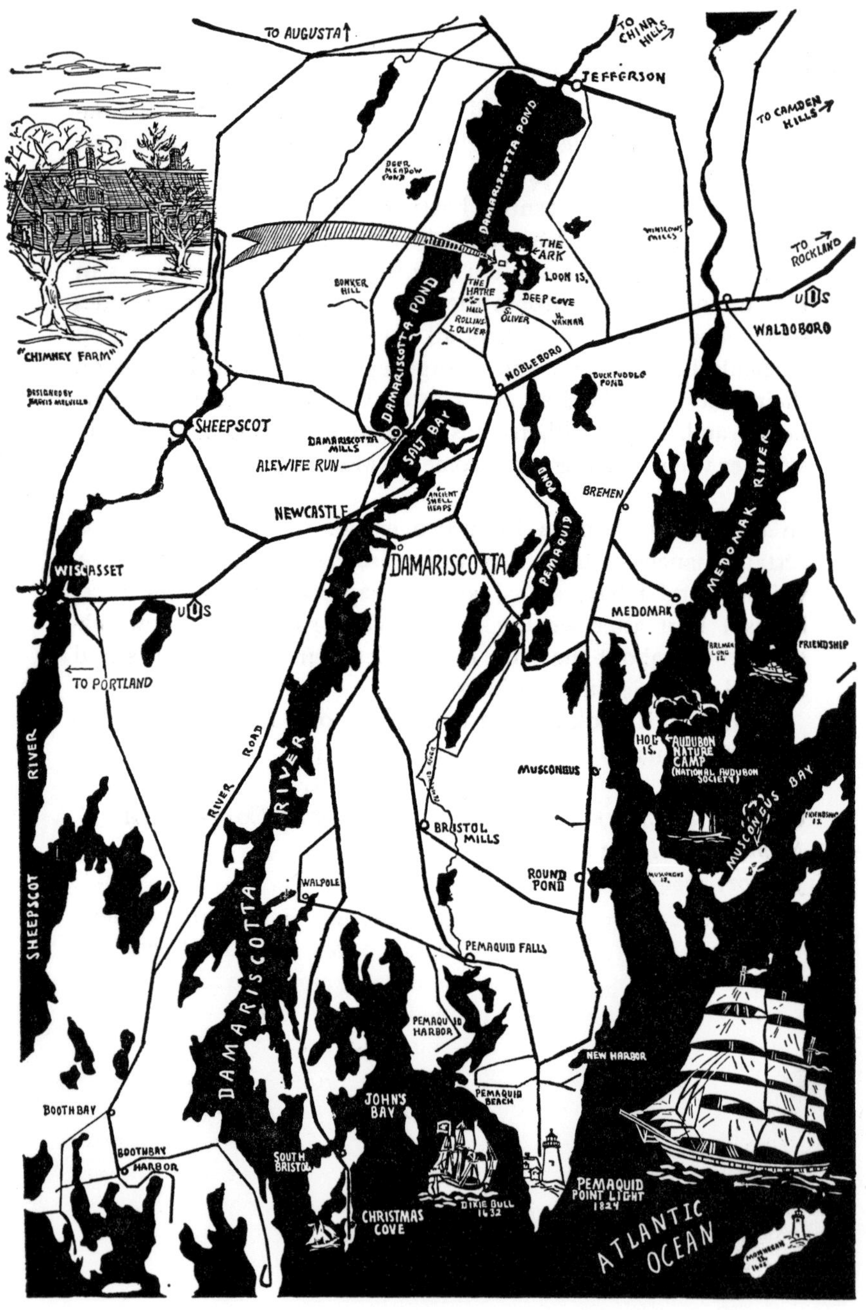
TO AUGUSTA
TO CHINA HILLS
JEFFERSON
TO CAMDEN HILLS
DAMARISCOTTA POND
DEER MEADOW POND
WINSLOWS MILLS
THE ARK
LOON IS.
TO ROCKLAND
BUNKER HILL
THE HATHE
HALL
ROLLINS
I. OLIVER
DEEP COVE
S. OLIVER
H. VANNAH
WALDOBORO
"CHIMNEY FARM"
NOBLEBORO
DUCK PUDDLE POND
SHEEPSCOT
DAMARISCOTTA MILLS
ALEWIFE RUN
SALT BAY
ANCIENT SHELL HEAPS
NEWCASTLE
BREMEN
MEDOMAK RIVER
DAMARISCOTTA
PEMAQUID POND
WISCASSET
MEDOMAK
FRIENDSHIP
TO PORTLAND
HOG IS.
AUDUBON NATURE CAMP (NATIONAL AUDUBON SOCIETY)
SHEEPSCOT RIVER
RIVER ROAD
DAMARISCOTTA RIVER
MUSCONGUS
MUSCONGUS BAY
BRISTOL MILLS
ROUND POND
WALPOLE
PEMAQUID FALLS
PEMAQUID HARBOR
NEW HARBOR
PEMAQUID BEACH
BOOTHBAY
JOHN'S BAY
BOOTHBAY HARBOR
SOUTH BRISTOL
CHRISTMAS COVE
DIXIE BULL 1632
PEMAQUID POINT LIGHT 1824
ATLANTIC OCEAN

Day at Chimney Farm

THERE IS a brightening at the windows, perhaps a slight stir in the house. If it is early summer, birds are singing, and it may be that the detestable phoebe is calling from the old high-top apple tree outside my windows. The door to the study is open, and through it the sunlight shines, making a yellow rug upon the floor. From where I lie, I cannot see the sun or the pond over which it shines or the woods along its shores; but I know that they are all there lying as though cupped in the palm of a great hand. My two bedroom windows to the south show only the boughs of apple trees, and the open door leads down to grass and trees, by three steps, up which a visiting porcupine occasionally climbs. The window at the foot of my bed looks northward over the herb garden and the chokecherry thicket which walls it in, but I cannot see out of it from the bed.

It is a pleasant room to wake in. The wallpaper is very fresh-looking, a calico sort of design, bad in detail, but very becoming to the walls. Beyond my bedside table the Parlor Gothic stove stands under the mantel. Opposite is an old bureau, and a dressing table fills the space between the two windows. One door opens into Henry's room, and another, in the same corner, reaches the clothes closet and Kate's room beyond. There are three downstairs bedrooms at the farm, a most unusual number, but we are fortunate because sometime about 1860 a married son added the "east house" to the main dwelling, and in it several generations were raised. This bedroom was once kitchen and general living room: the study beyond was the parents' bedroom, although it would seem to me scarcely wide enough for a bed, and in the attic overhead (where now Henry keeps his long shelves of books, a desk under a new dormer for rainy days, and a spare bed beyond a little stove) the children of this part of the farm once slept.

The past colors the present, faintly it is true. But lives leave some residue of emotion behind them. I like to live in rooms which have been seasoned by human experiences for a hundred years. If it is fall I shall hear the apples dropping occasionally from the old trees planted when the main story-and-a-half house was first built in the 1830's, and the bluebirds will pass giving their autumn call.

If I wake on a winter's morning, having obstinately clung to my own room and refused to move inward towards the warm center of the house as I sometimes do, it will be to a strangely pure and cold atmosphere. Long ago sometime in the night the last of the fire in the stove has burned out and the last red light has ceased to dance through the cracks of the cast iron and up along the ceiling. The room will be very cold. The windows are furred with a white hoarfrost nearly half an inch thick, through which the morning light shines strangely. If a glass of water has been left on the table beside the bed, it is crusted with ice. And yet I am warm between feather bed and blankets, warm with a peculiar felicity. To be warm in a warm room is nothing; but to be warm in an icily cold room is to taste a very special pleasure, a security in danger, peace in a storm.

"Don't bother to light the fire in here. I'll dress in the kitchen," I call as Henry appears at the door wearing his old wool bathrobe, a basket of kindling in his hand.

There is a coal fire in the dining room which has burned through the night and has just been replenished. In the big kitchen range the billets are snapping and sighing in the firebox and the coffee is already boiling. At this time of the year we seldom have a housekeeper, and our two daughters are at boarding school. I set the kitchen table by the western windows looking up towards the farm's high land with its pines. The tablecloth is checked. The dishes are gay. We have many arrangements of dishes which we enjoy using. Henry has already started the coffee, and I now make toast over the fire, lifting one of the stove's lids so that the living flames heat and brown the slices of bread. Perhaps a rasher or two of bacon add their sizzle and fragrance to the kitchen air.

Later, as I wash the dishes, I look downward from the wide expanse of window above the sink. The hayfields are under deep snow, and the pond has closed the marble lid of its eye and now seems only a level field where the wind patterns the old snow. Loon Island is no longer a dark ship moored in the bay. It seems a ridge rising above an unfenced meadow. Where are the loons which have nested there for as long as anyone can remember? Gone, and gone are all the birds, even the crows. On most days we shall see no living thing from any of our windows; but then unexpectedly a blue jay will call or a squirrel run along a stone wall, and when we walk in the woods we shall find ourselves surrounded by a tale of tracks of rabbits and mice and fox and partridge and deer, and know that we have secret neighbors whom we do not see, and that the drama of life and death goes on intensely behind the screen of trees and rocks.

The dishwater has been pumped at the sink from the cistern and heated on the stove, a slightly clumsy method and yet one to which I easily have become accustomed. There are the lamp chimneys to be done as well as the dishes, and then I like to burn the trash early, before the breeze comes to break the first stillness of the day. The air is so dry and motionless that I have often gone out without bothering to put on a sweater when the thermometer stood at 5 below zero. As the column of smoke billows up from the wire incinerator I glance about. Across the pond I can see the occasional farms, and smoke rises like a ghostly tree from each chimney, first in a straight trunk and then branching out in the slight currents of the upper air. It is beautiful with an unearthly beauty: the day will never again achieve this crystal calm.

Henry passes by, dressed in his warmest wools, a pail in his hand. He is going to the springhouse for drinking water. The upper and lower hatches will be lifted and the blue enamel pail tumbled on its length of rope into the shadowed pool through which one can see the rock basin so clearly. When he has hauled up the pail he too will stand looking about him.

I return to the housework. Why, with only snow on the ground, does so much dirt make its way every day into the house? Well, they say wood brings dirt, and certainly the hods of coal bring dirt, and the blankets seem to shed forever. The used part of the house is swept out every day; but the used part has shrunk: the kitchen, of course. Then comes the green dining room, with its big many-paned window looking out on the sun porch where we have most of our meals in summer. At this time of the year we eat only occasionally in the dining room or read at its round table in the evenings. It is a great temptation to pile it with things not wanted elsewhere. No. I carry an armful of books into Kate's cold room, put them on the little melodeon and close the door quickly. The parlor door need not be opened at all. Its rosy wallpaper and Victorian furniture await a summer rebirth. The upstairs bedrooms and bath may likewise be ignored, but I will make a foray into the arctic hallway and dust the upright piano, for, cold or no cold, Henry will go to it half a dozen times during the day and play some snatch of opera or hymn.

By now Henry's bedroom, opening from the dining room, is fairly warm by winter standards. I must smooth the mattress pad and sheet once more over the buffalo robe which now covers the mattress, for long ago we found that more chill comes up from below a bed than from above.

I hear an outside door open and shut, and the stamp of Henry's feet knocking off snow in the entry. He is bringing in a basket of kindling from the hillock piled up in the barn. What about half a cup of coffee?

So the morning work goes. We are survivors in a world of ice and snow. Unless we go visiting on our snowshoes we shall probably see no one all day long. Most of the canned goods in the pantry were brought there while the roads were open, but our milk and bread, our eggs and meat and fruit and vegetables have been carried in packsacks on our own backs at least as far as from the next farm, and oftener from the crossroads three quarters of a mile away. Each meal is a Robinson Crusoe triumph. Who would have guessed that made-over dishes could taste so good on the second, or on the third or even fourth appearance?

By the middle of the morning we are probably sitting opposite one another once more at the kitchen table; but now we are writing, perhaps letters, perhaps an article or book. Sometimes one of us will take work into the dining room instead, but we prefer the winter kitchen. Already the sun is high, and something is on the stove for the midday meal. The days are peaceful here beyond the end of the road, but they seem to go very fast. We have at present no telephone, no radio. We must amuse ourselves and one another. There are plans for snowshoeing across the lake in the afternoon, or perhaps we shall go visiting, or we are to drive with someone to the village store. Already it is suppertime, and then the dishes are washed, and if I am lucky Henry is reading aloud while I darn socks and stockings. Our supply of books seems almost inexhaustible. Henry has stored away all sorts and conditions of books in long shelves running nearly the whole length of the herb attic. And there are others in half a dozen places about the house as well.

Occasionally we have been at the farm during a real blizzard and have looked out to see the partridges sitting like smaller hens in our old apple trees eating the buds. The snow howls past, the drifts pile up, and we keep opening the storm doors to make sure that they will not become blocked, although the sliding doors of the woodshed would always make an egress if necessary. Then, when the storm is over, with what delight do we emerge into the blinding sunlight and deep swansdown! If the wind dropped before the snow stopped falling, our trees are white against a sky dark blue by contrast. We seem to be part of an upside-down world because the light has sunk to the bottom and the darker values lie now all about our heads.

Certainly we are out of touch with the world here in snow-time. But many of our happiest memories are winter memories. Each day is a sort of triumph. It takes so much effort and planning merely to exist and keep warm. But see, we have been comfortable, we have been content! And each night we go to our beds with a sense of having truly lived that day.

The Neighborhood

CHIMNEY FARM lies on the east slope of a point, or, as it is here called, a neck, stretching out into one of the three terminal bays of Damariscotta Pond. The old-timers still call it "pond" but on the maps it appears as "lake" and people here use the terms interchangeably, as the swamp on one side of the road as you come to East Neck is still called the Hathe by the older generation, which may well be the early English pronunciation for "heath." We like the phrase and still use it, thinking it has more suggestions than swamp, but swamp or hathe, it is the hollow bowl of a filled-in pond with sluggish water among the bushes where the muskrats build their tepees, and the peepers sing their first spring choruses in the dusk.

There are three farms on East Neck, and ours, the middle one, like the others is surrounded by hayfields looking east to the water with pasture land above, largely overgrown now; beyond that, woodland stretches down to Deep Cove on the west. The neighborhood is entirely given over to farming: the farms are not rich, for the soil is not rich. The population has shrunk, and the woods are webbing in the corners of the fields: old cellar holes and lost orchards and gravestones among the pines bear testimony to this.

But the people on this back road which is almost impassable in mud-time retain the old independent self-respecting Yankee tradition. While here and there the blood has run out and families like plants have gone to seed, the men and women of our township are for the most part people of character and breeding, not cut out of any one pattern as by machinery, but whittled and showing the grain. Among them you will find some of the oldest names in the history of New England, mixed with the names of the Germans who settled in the neighboring town of Waldoboro in the mid-eighteenth century. Our road with its small weather-beaten farms has in the last few years taken on a new hopefulness, that fundamental and basic hopefulness of birth. One day we counted thirty-six children in its scattered houses where twenty years ago there were only two along its three miles; for the East Neck Road is of course only a side road starting at the Nobleboro post office and running to our gate, where it changes into a lane for us and the Hall farm, then into a wood-road, and so veins out into dim trails leading to the water.

Our town is a very scattered one. Only the post office, one store, a church, the small anonymous town-office building, a school, three or four houses, and an obelisk to Arthur Noble mark its nucleus. Many people drive through it without suspecting that they have gone through a town at all; but it is an old town for Maine, settled in the eighteenth century as soon as the French and Indian Wars were over.

For a wonder we are not on a river, like most of our neighbor towns which grew up at the head of navigation on the great salt rivers which lie like arrows in a quiver, side by side: the Georges, the Medomak, the Damariscotta, the Sheepscot, the Kennebec, beautiful rivers with beautiful names. Sprinkled in the rivers and along the shores are innumerable islands, and inland there are innumerable lakes. So that even here in the farming country we see the sea gulls coasting along the old pasture lands looking for blueberries in July, and watch the sea haze blow in and hang upright on our horizon. On damp days when the wind is southeasterly, we can occasionally hear the foghorn at Pemaquid Point, and on a beam in the old barn of the farm next door someone long ago carved the outline of a schooner under full sail.

To either side of Nobleboro were ship-building and ship-sailing towns, although on our own road few of the men seem to have gone to sea. It is rather to the woods that the farmers' imaginations turn, and as surely as fall comes the young men oil their guns to go see if they can get them a deer, perhaps in their own wood lot but preferably farther off. Taking along a tent or an old trailer, they start out for the back country with a friend or two for company. They wear checked wool shirts, trousers laced in at the knee, high boots, and long red wool socks. The expedition is always a success, whether they bring back a deer or not, for they like the return to the pioneer conditions of their ancestors, and now they have new stories to tell around the stove.

From the Ark

IT WAS on a day early in May that we came to the Ark. Henry insisted that we should reach it for the first time by water; so we drove to the Mills with the supplies for our stay piled in the Days' car, and there hired a boat with an outboard motor and an elderly "captain" accustomed to take fishermen down the pond in search for landlocked salmon, or black bass, failing salmon.

As we chugged slowly along the tentacle of water which curls off from the main lake for four or five miles to the Mills, I watched the hilly shores on either side with their variegated pattern of farmland and woods, and the narrow islands which at a distance have the look of schooners in an anchorage. As we swung into the wider reaches of the main lake with the China Hills in the distance, my enthusiasm grew. A loon watched us, a great brightly colored bird, curious and attentive. When it had seen enough it dived from sight, reappearing a long time afterward, much farther away. I had not yet heard the wild ululation of its call to which I was so often to listen in the darkness of a night before rain, but already I was vaguely aware that here was one of the guardians of these waters.

We had turned now into a green bay between woods. Two islands lay at its entrance, and beyond to the right was a glimpse of beach; but our eyes were fixed mostly on the slopes to the left, which in two places showed the long scars of recent cutting-over. The slashes were, however, relieved by stretches of untouched pines and hemlocks crowding close to the water's edge.

"That's part of the farm," Henry said, keeping the excitement out of his voice.

Now the bay turned at right angles like the foot of a Christmas stocking. Gone were the distant islands and the more distant blue hills. Here only unstirred water lay in a deep fold of forested slopes, for these trees were not woodland trees but forest trees, many of them first-growth pines reaching up and up towards that incomparable sheer wall of cliff which we were later to call the Chinese Wall.

Not a house, not a trail, not a sign of man nor his work touched the purity of the scene, except that in the center of the pine-reflecting water lay a boat, such as a child might dream of. It was shaped like a toy Noah's Ark, with a narrow deck along its sides that widened at the bow. Low, many-paned windows with curtains drawn back lined most of the walls; but the roof, instead of being peaked, was flat, and a convenient ladder led up to it, a place from which to dive for those who liked diving, and for stargazing for those who might prefer stargazing.

As we thundered into Deep Cove, filling all the hollow places with the racket of our engine, we must have guessed that it was a place of echoes, where later we should hear the call of a thrush returned, and our own shouts tossed back to us in a cascade of cries, each one fainter and farther off than its fellow. A place of echoes and of reflections: I shall never forget the Ark in that early May. The old captain helped us to unload the bags and baskets of supplies. Then he brought us the rowboat which was moored to a solitary landing with a lantern on a pole beside it, and so left us to our borrowed kingdom.

At that time the Ark was, I think, only a year old. It had been built at the Mills, and the Days' idea was that they would have it towed to different parts of the lake and spend a few weeks or months now in this cove and now in that. But once they had taken possession of Deep Cove they were never able to move on. For one thing they never wanted to, and for another they lost the anchor next year, so that they were forced to moor alongshore; and later still, leaks began to appear and the Ark had to remain grounded in what had been its original winter quarters at the head of the cove, where the stream had spread a little meadow for the Rollinses' cows and the deer and occasional moose.

But when we landed on the Ark that May, lost anchors and leaks in the scowlike underhull were things far off in the impenetrable future. The vessel rode its mirror of water serenely. Eagerly as children we went down the three or four steps into the interior.

I suppose no woman ever grows too old to love a doll's house; and I have heard wives declare that their husbands' passion for sailing-boats was more than half due to the fun the men have keeping house in a little cabin. The Ark had all the doll's-house quality, but it was large enough so that one did not feel cramped in it on a rainy day. We entered a single long room with windows on either side and two doors and a bookcase along its back. A neat, beguiling sink to our right was overhung by dish shelves. Then came a wood stove, a huge copper kettle filled with dry wood beside it, and a table folding down below the windows with four canvas-seated chairs drawn up to it. Under the bookcase there was another table, with a jug of lilacs and magazines; and a couch stood beneath the windows to the left, with a small jog beyond for the toilet-room, on whose outer wall hung raincoats and fishing hats. The two doors flanking the bookcase led into two cabins, each with a large window, a double lower berth, a single upper berth that had its own small high window, and a rounded shelf and mirror in the remaining corner.

Such was and is the working plan of the Ark; but to know its quality one should know the details, the orderliness with which all the cooking things are fitted into their places, the charm of the hooks made from hard peeled crotches of wood, the pattern of the madras cotton on the couch, the amusing wooden birds and animals along the bookcase shelf which come from Jake's own workroom in the shed of the old house in Damariscotta, where he amuses himself when tired with painting and illustrating. It had taken the combined practical sense and poetry of Jake and Bee to create the Ark.

I forget some of the details of our lives for the next ten days. I think that the Days once came from town to see us and brought us fresh supplies. Was it every day or every other day that we rowed to the wharf, moored our boat, and walked through the thrush-haunted woods into the Rollinses' pasture—which was then misted over with the lovely little flower called bluets or quaker-ladies—and so, keeping carefully to the path so as not to spoil the young hay, reached the Rollinses' house for half an hour's talk in the kitchen, fresh milk in a pail, fresh eggs in a basket, and two glass cider jugs filled with well water? We carried the jugs on leather straps easier for the hand than any handle, and I remember that Henry was proud of me on the evening when I first guided our expedition safely back to the waiting rowboat through the darkness along a thread of trail.

We had not been married quite two years at the time, and I was still making excuses to say "my husband." It sounded so pleasant, and still does. "We" is a much wider-open door than "I." You see a good deal more of life from it, a brighter landscape, a wider view. Henry is particularly good at widening a wife's view because he knows everything—knows the names of constellations even when they appear upside down in their inconsequential way, knows the names of birds and of all historical characters, knows books and living people and why they do what they do. This is wonderfully arousing in certain aspects, and convenient in others for a woman with a short memory; but it's particularly nice to have so much scholarship stored away in a person full of warmth and wit. All the same, he hasn't a strong sense of direction in the woods, and his favorite cry in strange hotels is "Lead, kindly wife."

But if he will never make a Maine guide, he has a Napoleonic quickness and sureness of decision. He had been at Damariscotta visiting the Days the month before, and on his way back from a weekend at the Ark had heard Jake accosted by an old farmer who was walking past their car, stuck deep at the moment in the ruts of mud-time:

"Know anyone who'd like to buy my farm, Mr. Day?"

"No, I don't, Mr. Bennett."

"It's next to the Rollinses on East Neck," Jake explained later to Henry.

And Henry thought, "*I'd* like to buy it."

He told me about it while we were having a fish luncheon at a Quincy restaurant. He drew rough plans of East Neck and Deep Cove on a menu. He had never set foot on the land, but he liked the district, the feel of the lake and countryside. He had no need to go shopping, to look at this town house or that cottage on a salt river, to weigh the hills of Vermont against the elms of Connecticut.

Casually, carelessly, but surely, he chose the place he wanted for a home. He had only seen the farmhouse at a distance, so much in need of paint and so disfigured by added accretions of plank verandas that he had thought it would have to be torn down. He drew dreadful pictures of it on the menu, which the house today would not care to see.

So that was why we were on the Ark, cooking our meals, sweeping our doll's house, swimming on the warm afternoons, walking through the woods to the Rollinses'.

It was not until the third day that Henry rowed me over to a very small beach against a wall of pine boughs which swung open to the beginnings of a path. "Betsy's Landing," he named it as I stepped ashore, for the first time setting foot on what was to be, by the end of another week, our land.

Then we received a telegram from a banker friend:

"We have met the Bennetts and they are ours—map, vane, and manure pile."

And so the farm became ours, so far as human beings may ever possess the aged granite, and the pine and beech growing by their own fierce will to live, and the hay striving to keep its place against the forest, and passing creatures which take up their residence there for a season: the pileated woodpeckers of our slash; the doe with her two fawns at this moment wandering our woods; the porcupines whose paths no longer lead to our apple trees because this summer there are no apples; the many birds. All these things, some as old as the earth, and some with only a few hours' span of life, are not really ours except by a kind of legal quibble. The farm in one form or another will outlive all its masters and man himself. But we do own the house and the barn and the stone walls and the fruit trees. They were made by man's will and are dependent upon us. The house should be rather grateful to us, I think, for its pleasant lines of the 1830's had been much disfigured and, although we have not tried to turn the clock back to the original form, we have remade its harmony.

The telegram referred specifically to three objects of value which might be removed, or so we thought.

The map is a simple surveyor's map which shows the Neck, and the division of 1827, made by the original settler who divided his land between his two sons. There are walls between our land and the Rollinses' to the south; but only between the hayfields were walls ever erected along the boundaries of the farms of the two Hall sons, and the cattle of both roamed the same pastures, and the oxen dragging out firewood or timber for new sills used the same wood-roads. When we had finally signed our papers at the bank, Mr. Bennett took us over the bounds. I remember what a fine autumn day it was, and how exciting we found the scramble through the woods, up and down, now along half-open glades, now through thickets, making beelines from one line tree to another.

Later we were to return many times to the old rye field, which in time we called Meg's Meadow after our elder daughter. The sumac and juniper were beginning to encroach upon it, and the next autumn old Mr. Rollins and his son-in-law worked there clearing it. Henry and I walked down one afternoon to help drag branches to the fire, which was burning with a heavy, almost ponderable smoke changing from green to sulphur-yellow and tarnish-black, then to opalescent rose and blue. We fell into talk as we watched the slow-changing column of vapor twisting upward in a baroque column. Mr. Rollins told us that he had seen thirty men at work in that rye field when our farm had been getting out its lumber.

"All the neighbors here and across the lake came. We sawed wood and split it all afternoon. Most of the time someone was telling a story or a joke, and then about five o'clock the women came down and we had a baked-bean supper right here with pies and cakes and brown bread. It was what used to be called a chopping bee. People had more fun in those days."

"We'd better show them what we found," said Carroll, the son-in-law. And he led us to the edge of the big pines where two narrow slabs of slate were driven into the ground some four feet apart.

"Probably a child was buried here before they began the graveyard above your place. They always say this was the first cleared land on the Neck."

"Yes," said Mr. Rollins. "When you work in the woods around where the early houses stood, you find graves marked like this, often two or three of them together. Once in a while they've scratched initials or a date on the stone, but usually it's plain like these."

We looked down at the anonymous little grave. Is a boy or girl buried there? We shall never know, but the oblong field in the heart of the pines has an added sentiment because of the child's bones lying in it, and it is curious that not far away grows a bed of the only white everlasting flowers I have seen in this part of the country.

That late October day, there was even more to show us.

"You tell what you saw, Carroll," said Mr. Rollins.

Carroll stopped to wipe his hot face on the sleeve of his blue shirt.

"No, you tell."

"No, you tell, Carroll. You found it."

"Well, I saw a moose track this morning on the road."

Henry and I exclaimed.

A moose in our own woods!

"It wasn't a big one," Carroll went on, "not more than a two-year-old, I guess." And he led us to the track, not unlike a cow's, and pointed out the mark made by the tips of the hooves, which had not been worn off (showing that the creature was young) and were not spread far apart (showing that the animal was not yet heavy).

So much for the map. The weathervane, made by some friend of the original family out of a sheet of tin, became at once a great favorite of mine. It shows a rider on a galloping horse, reins in one hand, whip in the other. He wears a jockey cap. I call him Johnny-Ride-the-Sky and always look to him when I wish to see which way the wind is blowing; but Henry thinks that age has made him untrustworthy.

"He is riding yesterday's wind," Henry declares.

"No!" I cry, vindicating Johnny. "Here on the lake the wind comes from two ways, and he is riding the one at his level."

It is perfectly true that our skies often show two layers of clouds moving in opposite directions, one from the sea and one from the land. They meet and form all sorts of cloud shapes, to Henry's continual delight. Sometimes a bank of fog hangs along the edge of our southern sky, and thunderheads foam and tower to the north, making a hundred forays and excursions upon one another's territories. Johnny-Ride-the-Sky does the best he can, often with a bird seated on his head or on the hand which holds the reins. My best writing paper has his silhouette at the top of the page, for he represents all this broad expanse of sky which we so much love, where the northern lights dance in the autumn, paling Capella above our neighbor's barn, and the Milky Way flows over our roof guiding our lane onward towards Scorpio, large and straggling above the Hathe, where it lies unseen, dark, and secret. Over the oak grove to the northwest the Great Dipper swings slowly on its handle, and from the lake we watch lazy Orion emerge, recumbent, first showing only a knee and glittering shoulder and then at last his sword. These are the companions of Johnny-Ride-the-Sky.

As for the manure pile for which we bargained, I do not go near it very often, as it stands in an old barnyard overgrown with raspberry bushes which have many thorns but few raspberries. Grass and weeds grow very thick on the hillock which was once the manure pile, and at one time two big snakes were fond of lying there to warm their cold sides between the sun and the manure, which returned the sun's heat, Henry tells me. But long ago the haymakers killed one of the snakes, and an Indian coming here to sell baskets killed its mate a few weeks later. So the great snakes are gone, to startle me no more, and their mysterious and dignified presences have departed from our walls and the manure pile for which we bargained, but which, like so many things, we did not greatly value in possession.

But, coming upon that fateful telegram, I had a sudden stir of memory, and a return to the mood of excitement in which we had waited to know whether or not we were indeed to become landholders:

"We have met the Bennetts and they are ours—map, vane, and manure pile."

Snowshoe Rabbit

IN WINTER, walking along our road, I often see the tracks of rabbits in the snow, the small front paws and the long hind paws coming together in a cluster which is shaped like a butterfly. When we walk in the woods, these tracks are often so close together that we say, "There's been a rabbit ball last night." But only once have I seen an actual snowshoe rabbit.

That winter I was writing a novel, *An Incredible Tale,* in which one of these rabbits played a pivotal part in the action. He represented the magical powers of an Indian medicine man, long since dead, or possibly of his son, still alive and concerned with the disintegration of a white household living on a lonely hill-farm.

On this particular morning I had been writing about the coming of this animal and of the effect it had had upon the rather disturbed young son of the family. Then it was time to go shopping and I laid aside paper and pen to drive to Damariscotta with Henry. The road had been recently plowed and there were high clean snowbanks on either side. We drove the first two miles without incident, down the hill to the railroad track, and started up the opposite hill. On the right side there is a small gravel pit, on the left young thick-growing pines which have usurped a former hayfield. At the top of the hill stands the house where long ago the two sons were taken desperately ill. One died, but the life of the other was saved by a passing Indian medicine man. It was this man who was the original of the Indian in my story. So no spot in our countryside could have been more appropriate than this for the apparition which now appeared. At first I could scarcely believe that I really was seeing what I thought I saw.

"Henry, do you see what I see?" I demanded.

"Yes," he said, "a snowshoe rabbit."

There the big creature lay, unstirring, on the top of the snowbank to the left of the road. I could see its bulging dark eyes watching us serenely. Its coat was white, save for twin dark spots of brown at the tips of its long ears, matching its eyes.

In winter our back roads are narrow after being plowed, but the rabbit never moved as we drove by within three feet of it. Even when we were beyond it, it made no effort to cross the road. Looking back, I could still see it, as white as the mounded snowbank on which it lay, save for its four accents of brown.

From that day to this, I have never seen another snowshoe rabbit. Call it coincidence if you like, but it still seems as incredible to me as anything I had been conjuring up in my tale.

Keeping Eskimos

FRANCES is one of the best story-tellers I have ever known, racy, humorous, tolerant, and pitying. She lives in a nearby town which for me flashes with light from a thousand strange facets:

"I first saw her one day on the train. I couldn't help noticing that she was reading a French book and was middle-aged and very well dressed. We got into talk, and she told me that she lived all by herself in a house in the woods: it was only later I heard that years ago she'd been run out of town . . .

" 'Yes,' my tenant remarked, 'that man walks too straight to be honest.' And at that time he was greatly respected by everyone. It was only much later that it came out . . .

"They hadn't spoken for years but that night the neighbors heard scream after scream from his room . . .

"And she insisted on going to the church in a taxi, although the church was only a block from the house. It wouldn't do to have the groom call for her in his car, either. He mustn't see the bride on their wedding day, you know—even if they *had* been already living together all winter . . .

"And she called out: 'Damn you! Come in.' And when she saw it was a neighbor she said: 'Oh, excuse me! I thought it was Mother.'

"So at last the professor put his head out of the window and yelled, 'My God, madam, can't you remember that you're a widow?' "

I remember the stories, or sometimes only snatches of them, each a New England novel compressed into five minutes of talk over a teacup. But most of these stories are a little too urban and recent for my use. I like the tale which has been stored like an apple in the attic, and has felt the cold of winter cracking the shingles overhead and heard the big stupid black flies of spring bumbling and bungling at the dusty windows. Perhaps I like fields in the picture. The houses of a town, even a little town, come too close: the lines warp one another into bitter shapes. These thwarted, desperate, funny stories have not the quiet comedy and tragedy in them that our true farm stories keep. Here we are nearer the other world of wonder, the cows low for milking, the fox barks from the autumn woods, there is a ring around the moon.

But this friend knows country stories, too. She took us one day for a picnic on a road which was barely passable. It was hard to believe that this lane dipping down to streams in the wood, veering over rocky ledges, had once been the stagecoach road; and it was not easy to think that the little deserted red-brick building opposite the graveyard at a forgotten crossing had ever been a tavern.

But she assured us that it had. We took out our rugs and picnic things and spread them in the sun. There were apples very bright on the old trees, and the biggest and most perfect spiderwebs I have ever seen were spread across the open doorways of the gray sheds. The inevitable chipmunk came chittering and scolding along a stone wall, and the crickets were making their usual scarcely heard chorus.

We walked about the little building, past the clumps of lilacs, and climbed on a cellar bulkhead, trying to peer through a shutter into the dark interior.

The bulkhead reminded Frances of something.

"It was down here," she remarked casually, "that they kept the Eskimos that winter."

It was as though she had said, "In this room they boarded the tiger." Not of course that Eskimos are dangerous; but here in these deserted fields they seemed as exotic as anything from the jungle. I looked at the little tavern with a new excitement. Only two or three narrow peeps of glass lighted whatever cellar there was under the house; but Frances said that the Eskimos preferred it to a room. It must have been more like an igloo.

I have read the story since with names and dates and later happenings, but I prefer to remember it as Frances told it while we unpacked the picnic basket in the late September sunshine. It took place in that wonderful time "when the old people I first knew here were children." Some vessel—was it a sealer?—had found a group of Eskimos on an ice floe, drifting south; I rather think there was a white man with them, an English explorer. Anyway, there were several Eskimo men with their women, and two or three children as well. They were taken aboard, and then the question arose as to what to do with them, as it was too late in the season to go north again to any land they knew. The skipper agreed to take them with him in the spring when he went sealing again. Meanwhile he suggested this old tavern, where he could make arrangements, and the winter was likely to be cold enough to keep the Arctic visitors comfortable.

And so it turned out. They lived for months in this dark hole about which we prowled. I wonder if they built an entrance to it of packed snow, and whether they were given whale oil to burn in its icy depths? At least none of them died. And the old people of the town, who then were children, remember the Eskimos walking occasionally into the village to make a few simple purchases, wearing their fur-trimmed parkas and sealskin boots, and still tell how round-faced and bright-eyed the children were.

And then in the spring they sailed away, and the memory of them became a legend and things were dated for a while from "the winter the Eskimos were here," and gradually they were forgotten as a visit of Arctic owls would be forgotten; but Frances had heard the story from people who had seen them, and she told it to me just as I am telling it to you.

Bricks

"THE BRICKS for the chimneys on East Neck were made at the place where you go swimming," said Marion. "All the farms got their bricks there." We had not known that, although we had seen the place where the great stones for the farm's foundations had been split from the rocky outcrops of what had been the pasture, but is now forest again. The sills and beams and clapboards had certainly come from the wood lot. We realized that our farm was part of its own earth, except for the windows and ironware which would have had to be bought.

What is true of Chimney Farm is probably true of most of the early farmhouses of Maine. Their ingenious builders used the materials at hand and employed the varied skills which the men seem to have taken for granted.

At Damariscotta all the stores on both sides of the street are built of brick and there are a few brick houses, all using the local material made in the brickyards along the river. People have told me that most of Back Bay in Boston was built with Damariscotta River bricks.

One morning, I was sitting in the car waiting while Henry did an errand when old Mr. Lindsay, the photographer, came by and stopped for a talk. The subject turned to brickyards.

"There were twenty-three or twenty-four of them on the river," he told me. "They made bricks during the summer. Usually there was a pond or reservoir above the yard with a trickle of water coming down and an old horse or mule would be driven round and round to mix the clay with water. They had forms. They'd press the clay down, then smooth it off with a board and, when it had partly dried, they would carefully slip out the damp gray bricks to dry some more.

"In the fall they'd fire them. They had great piles of cordwood which they kept stoking day and night in those big ovens under the bricks. We boys used to go down on a moonlit fall night and roast potatoes and corn at some kiln beside the river. The bricks turned red in the firing.

"Later in the fall, or sometimes it wouldn't be until next spring, the schooners would lie off the yards and put out a plank and we boys loaded the boards, ten bricks to a board with cleats at each end, three boards to the bottom of a wheelbarrow, ten boards to a wheelbarrow—that was a load. When the bricks were stacked on the schooners, they'd throw down the boards to the boys to repack. We used to get a few cents a thousand bricks. Perhaps eighty-three or eighty-five cents for a day's work.

"They were good bricks. Damariscotta is built of them, but when they began to make bricks by machinery in Massachusetts, the yards couldn't compete and one by one they closed."

How his talk brought back the times I have sailed down the river and the glimpses I have caught of some small cove with a jumble of broken bricks on the shore, half hidden by weeds! In such places the schooners had lain just offshore and the boys had toiled eagerly, trundling their hundred-brick wheelbarrows up the gangway plank.

It was some time later that a friend told me the story of one of these boys. His father owned a brickyard where the boy had worked, probably from the time he was twelve or thirteen. At last, when he was eighteen, he had succeeded in getting the permission of his family to go to Boston on one of the brick schooners.

This particular vessel was caught in a gale off the Isles of Shoals and wrecked and nothing further was heard of the boy. His family gave him up as lost, but many months later they had a letter from Brisbane. During the storm a vessel bound for Australia had picked him up on some piece of wreckage and then continued on her way, with no time to waste in putting a boy on shore at an American port. Once in Brisbane, he had liked the place and the people. His family never saw him again. He married an Australian and had a large Australian family. For a while letters were exchanged, but as the years went by, they became less and less frequent and at last stopped altogether.

So for the second time the son of the family was lost, and this time forever.

Foxes

IF ONE HAD three lovely daughters born on such a farm as ours, they might be named Sylvia, Echo, and Demeter. Their names would suggest the woodland, the rocky echo-haunted heights, and the sloping fields combined in these farms, where the wild and the tame are in continual interplay like shadows of leafy branches in a wind.

Certainly the cows here have often met with deer and moose, and the late hay is filled with well-beaten little paths of porcupines visiting the apple trees about the houses, and on the fall evenings one listens to make certain whether it is a fox or a farm dog yapping in the distance. The fox seems to impress the imagination of every countryside where he is common, and appears as Br'er Fox, or Reynard in his monk's gown, or the ghost foxes of Japan, which can take the shape of beautiful women to beguile the lonely traveler.

Here there are no legends of foxes that I know of; but they do curious things and are noticed. Old Mr. and Mrs. Rollins looked out early one autumn morning and saw a big red fox sitting in the sunlight of the dooryard staring at their windows and lolling his tongue out and laughing.

"The impudence of him!" cried Mrs. Rollins, indignant even at the memory. "Howard went to get his shotgun, but before he could load it the fox went off, laughing at us still. I didn't like it, I tell you. He was so bold about it, like we were nothing to be afraid of."

"Has one ever come so near the house before?" I asked.

Mrs. Rollins thought. "Once when the old black cat was alive—you know, the one who could open doors and knew when a setting hen wasn't on her eggs. Well, I remember once looking out and seeing the old cat coming up the road with a fox following along after her, about four-five feet behind. Every time the fox came up nearer, the old cat would turn round spitting terrible, and that fox would kind of draw back. But you know they dearly love cat flesh. I went out and waved my dish-cloth, and Mr. Fox thought he'd better go off on his business."

Mr. Rollins spoke up from his big rocking chair with that air of slow deliberation which adds an importance to anything he says.

"Funny thing about foxes," he remarked meditatively. "They won't go near anything iron which a man has touched. I had a turkey once with a crooked foot, and she stole a nest at the edge of the woods. I found it, and I took out a chain—wagon trace, it was—and made a circle round the nest. But I was in a hurry to get back to dinner, and I didn't see to it that the ends quite met.

"Next morning I went to see how she was. She was gone, and every egg was broken and sucked. Only thing left was that crippled foot of hers. Fox had come right through the gap."

Last fall there was a fox in our neighborhood that screamed. "When the mists rise from the lake the foxes mate," the people hereabouts say. Walking by night down along the Hathe, before going to bed, we heard this screaming sound beyond us, and later were told that Paul, the caretaker at the sawmill, had met a fox on the road at dusk and it had screamed at him. Paul is a French Canadian, who has almost forgotten his native tongue after long solitary residence among Yankee neighbors. But I feel sure that old memories must have wakened in his mind, and northern stories of haunted spirits stirred at the back of his thoughts.

I have seen foxes often here, and still more often followed their busy interweaving tracks in new-fallen snow, and smelt their odor like old grapes. But there were two little foxes which I became well acquainted with. I remember driving up to our friends', the Days', house in the village on a May afternoon. The

Day boys were then perhaps twelve and fourteen years old, and somewhere they had found or been given a pair of very young fox cubs. A fisherman whose dory had been followed home by a baby seal, perhaps deserted by its mother, had given them the seal. Elsewhere they had acquired a wire-haired fox terrier puppy, a kitten, and a pair of big Belgian hares. The green dooryard was a perfect scene of the mingling of the wild and tame.

That morning the little seal had been taken in a wheelbarrow down to the cove half a block away for its day of swimming, but as usual it had grown hungry before it was called for again, and had flipper-flapped its way home along the concrete sidewalk, practically stopping traffic. I remember its fat baby face, its round eyes, and its whiskers which twisted in corkscrews. Bee Day was coaxing it away from the flower border with a fish while the two little foxes, with their pointed faces and big ears very large for their tiny bodies, dashed about through the tall grasses like excited demons. The puppy barked ecstatically, but it was the kitten which really played with the cubs, lying in wait for them, dashing out from ambush, to roll and scuffle with them on the warm earth. Seeing our amusement, the boys let out a big hare, which hopped about placidly, and then joined the sport by allowing the little foxes to chase it, and then chasing the cubs in turn, leaping over them in a great bound.

Suddenly there was a squeal of rage and a scuffle. A foxlet had smelled the fish which Neptune, the little seal, was eating. It had rushed upon the water-baby and had given it a sharp nip on the nose, seizing the piece of fish it coveted and running off into a thicket of grass to devour what it had stolen. Someone picked the culprit up by the scruff and cuffed it lightly.

"You ought to be ashamed! Poor Neptune!" The little seal looked upset and surprised, but forgot its troubles at the appearance of another herring.

The last time I saw either fox was some months later. Neptune had been returned to the sea. The kitten and puppy were living the immemorial lives of their kind; the rabbits were in a hutch. But the little foxes had been returned to the woods above Deep Cove. I had walked down to see the Days on their houseboat and had with me that big black pit-bull terrier called Bos'n who was for so long the household dog, the gentlest-hearted creature that ever drew breath—"an old dog saint," Henry used to call him—for all his warlike tradition. As Bee and I walked along the path by the edge of the cove we saw something golden-red flitting towards us from the cliffs, frisking among the pines. It was the little vixen, now almost full grown, who had heard Bee's voice and had come to meet her.

I caught Bos'n by the collar. The pretty fox came up to us, rolling on the path and playing a little like a dog, a little like a cat, but with a charming elfin gaiety which belongs to neither. When she reached us she came up to Bos'n, whom she had never seen before, and touched his nose with her delicate nose-tip. He whined, bewildered and enchanted, and she played about us confidently. For that moment, she was the spirit of the August woods, harmless and fearless, at peace with itself, and neither wild nor tame, but something beyond either.

Giving

THE DUNBARS were the first people to settle on the East Neck Road after the Halls, who built the big house next to us at the very end of the Neck sometime about the end of the eighteenth century. I never think of the Halls without being overwhelmed by the magnanimity of the human spirit that would build on so large and civilized a scale in the midst of bears and Indians; and not only did they build this great house with its many windows and fine doors, but they changed their minds about its location and moved it across the ice one winter and up the steep slope from the water to the commanding position it now holds. I wonder how many yoke of oxen were used and who drove them, and how they knew how to do it? But in Maine moving things boldly has always been a characteristic of the people. They say that the old German church at Waldoboro was stolen one winter's night from the north side of the river and set up again on the south side; where it still stands, although the north-siders must have been pretty mad about it for the first thirty or forty years. The Marie Antoinette house of Wiscasset was also moved across the wide Sheepscot in its time, and I have heard a tale of a good-sized schooner having been built well inland to be near the supply of white oaks, and then taken to the water hauled by oxen in the grand manner.

But the Dunbars did not move their low, early nineteenth-century house. It was built where it now stands, although Mrs. Dunbar tells me that the first Dunbar log cabin stood near the barn on the other side of the brook.

"He must have settled where he did account of the running water. Maybe that's why we find Indian things on our farm more than most places. There's not much running water hereabouts.

Probably that's what made that Indian who called himself Bedagi ask if he could camp here. Didn't you ever hear of him? It was when Lester was a little boy. He says those Indians were real good people. They wouldn't even pick up an apple off the ground without asking if they might. That must have been sixty or more years ago.

"The schoolhouse next door was used then of course, and Bedagi's children went to school there, a boy and a girl. There was a little one too, who died while they were here and was buried up in the corner of our graveyard. No, there wasn't a real stone, but I know the place. Haven't you ever heard of the entertainment Bedagi gave at the schoolhouse one evening? All the mothers and fathers of the pupils came—I guess anyone who wanted to, for that matter—and his little boy stood up across the room with an apple on his head, and Bedagi shot it off with an arrow. Then the little girl lay right down on the floor and there, before everyone's eyes, he threw knives around her and outlined her from head to heels. Gracious, I'm glad I wasn't there to see it."

Gentle Mrs. Dunbar, hardly taller than the cosmos which flowers everywhere for her! She has had four children, a daughter who lives at home and three sons now all grown up and away; but she seems like a little girl herself, unhardened by life. To her, birds and flowers are still the most important things she knows. She writes verses and gives people things: she walks the stony Maine roads to go neighboring, as it is called, always with a box of berries or a packet of flower seeds in her hand, or maybe some cookies she has just made, or a pincushion she has put together from some silk she came across. In a part of the world where everyone is generous, Mrs. Dunbar shines as the most generous of all, giving, giving, giving as naturally as a cricket chirrups or a chipmunk runs on a sunny wall. Because we had been talking of Indians, Mrs. Dunbar wanted to give me a little string of wampum which had been found near here. It was the only local wampum I have ever seen, and I failed in an equal generosity of acceptance. I could not bring myself to take more than three or four beads from one end. Only saints can give and take as freely as the elements come and go.

The Pond

DAMARISCOTTA POND is supposed to be about fourteen miles long, from the old and now disused sawmill at the top of our bay to the stream which enters it at the village of Jefferson. It is a charming body of water. We aren't fishermen, so I cannot say much about its landlocked salmon, its black bass, or its pickerel. I know that sometimes the young alewives will pass in a dark line about a foot wide following along the shore like a ribbon trembling as it is pulled through the water. We have watched it for ten or fifteen minutes at a time before the last alewife passed, remembering the beauty and sadness of the alewife run up the cascades at the Mills, while the eagles perch in the oaks along the shore, glutted with fish.

I say "sadness" because I know of nothing else which shows so clearly the almost insupportable effort which Nature demands of her children, and which they are able somehow to make. It takes an alewife about twenty-four hours to climb the stair of white water from pool to pool under the village willows. There are two branches of the stream. The fish which turn to the left towards the falls are doomed to be packed in no time in barrels of salt for the West Indies trade, or to be dried to a curious gold and strung on wands to be sold in our village groceries, or to be given to local widows according to the original charter.

But the fish which turn to the right will live, to reach their goal, the lake. I have stood on the little bridges which make this run so charming, and have looked down for as long as I could bear to do it, watching some especial alewife, marked perhaps by a scar of silver on its blue-black side, try again and again to make the four- or five-foot dash up to the next basin of circling water, thick with resting fish. Obviously they succeed, but after what failures! what exhaustions! Again and again my fish tries it, springs out of its wild shelter into the full white downrush of the stream, breasts it nobly with all the impetus of its effort, rises, rises one foot, two feet, perhaps three feet, the spirit driving on the body, and then is borne back, sideways, still struggling, to the basin it had hoped to leave.

There it swims for a while worn out, but not for long. Again you see the silver scar flash forward, again the fallible flesh flings itself against the terrible strength of the water, again it is defeated. But the roe must be born—who knows why it must be in a lake, and not in a river or in the sea where the schools live? But such is not the decree. My fish, with its side already scraped against some jagged rock against which it has been flung, must not give up trying until it succeeds or dies. There it goes again. Almost that trim dark shape reaches the next pool, but at the white lip it is torn down once more. By this time I can all but hear it scream.

After a while I suggest that we go up to the dam, at this time partly opened, and watch the successful alewives, which have only now to have their young and die in peace. Yes, they are there, one or two arriving at a time, breasting the last current, swimming slowly into the quiet lake water. They have to me a dazed air, as of creatures which have reached their goal by so hard a road that they have forgotten what they wanted. They swim slowly about, recovering, I suppose. Altogether, the run of alewives is a sight very wonderful and tragic. I cannot help but be reminded of what human beings suffer within the very simple framework of life—to be born, to find one's mate, to bring to life, and to die.

But, after all, our pond itself is not sad to look at nor to think about. Its variegated woodlands and farmlands are beautiful. It has hills and the promise of mountains beyond. From my window here I see on the high land across the water a little empty white farmhouse with two big arborvitae trees beside it; and sitting underneath those trees with a picnic basket, I have often looked up from unwrapping a covered dish of hot macaroni and cheese to see Mount Washington on the horizon. The swallows high above me at this moment can get an excellent view of the Camdens, going down in blue heights to the sea. So, although we actually see nothing higher than the China Hills from the lake, we know that we are but one remove from larger fry.

Our pond is prettily diversified by islands, coves, clean shores of stone and pine, and beguiling stretches of sheltered waters where the water lilies float, or the rushes rub against the sides of the canoe and the duck rise with a whistling of wings from their feeding. Below our own fields, we have seen moose tracks in March on the softened ice of the pond, but I have yet to meet with some great creature feeding on the roots of the yellow lilies, although others have seen that sight.

It is a little difficult to remember the past when on water, for water holds no trace of it. I have always known that the lumber rafts once came down the lake to the two sawmills, one here, and one at the Mills; but in our time the logs are towed a few at a time by a puffing old motorboat or come in trucks lurching along the road. Once in the late fall we met a big yoke of oxen coming single file over the ice bringing logs; but that was nothing to the forty or fifty yoke that Postmaster Sterling Oliver remembers seeing as a boy from the window of his house. The lake is not used much in winter nowadays: a little ice is cut in square green blocks, a few cars take short-cuts to their friends on the opposite shore; five winters ago a team was lost in a fault near Pint Pot Island just off our own shore. They had been working on this side of the lake, I forget now at what, and were going home to their farm across from us. In the middle of the pond, between the two islands, something went wrong. The ice buckled and broke under the heavy horses, and the man sprang back only just in time.

But it was not until Mrs. Hall came to help us last fall while Annie was home with a wrenched knee that I talked with someone who had known the lake intimately in its working days.

Both her father and her husband had been lumber dealers between Jefferson and Bunker Hill. She is quite an elderly woman, and she remembers how, when spring came on, her mother always made sure that she had some good strong new sheets. Then some morning long before dawn the rafts would put out, all along the shore, one or two from a farm. The logs were fastened together in a great oblong—not pointed into a prow—and two or three of the sheets were fastened, each between two poles ("No, they didn't tear," Mrs. Hall assured me), for impromptu sails. Each raft had at least two men with poles and a long steering sweep, and she and her mother would stand on the shore watching the moving lanterns and listening to the shouting of the men from raft to raft.

"Mother always packed up a big pail of food for each one of our rafts," Mrs. Hall told me. "She was a fine cook, and they used to send good hearty food with the men in those days. There'd be a cold roast of beef or pork, and a loaf or two of bread and a crock of butter and maybe a pound of cheese and pies baked the day before, and a cake or two. The men would get to the Mills sometime during the afternoon, and all drive back together. But the early start gave them good appetites, and my mother never stinted them."

Birds

THERE ARE a hundred accounts of the flocks of passenger pigeons which once passed like a dark cloud across the North American sky for hours on end, and by sheer weight of numbers broke branches from the great oaks where they lighted. I remember when I was a girl listening to an old Canadian farmer's talk, telling how tired as a boy he got each winter of eating pigeon. They were lightly pickled, barrel after barrel, and put away in the cellar, and I suppose his mother kept urging him, "Now, eat your pigeon like a good boy."

Alive they must have been beautiful, very like the three mourning doves that came to our feeding stand this year, but larger. No one in the world will see again their vast migrations, but I can remember three occasions when I have experienced something of this sense of the wealth and fecundity of natural life.

Every year for as far back as anyone could remember, the crows held their autumn convention at our farm. They seemed very conscious of property boundaries. It was not to the farms north or south of us that they came, but to ours, landing in the yellow tops of the old beech trees among the pines, but particularly blackening our mowed fields in which the soft young grass was at a convenient height. Here they would move in squadrons which numbered in the hundreds, always facing south as I remember, walking with the stately strut of an eighteenth-century landed proprietor surveying his property. They were glossy and shining, beautiful birds, with a noble assurance. People say that at these caucuses they sometimes try an offender, circling him with much cawing and then closing in and pecking him to death. We never witnessed anything of the kind, and I wonder what a crow crime would be? I can only think that such an unfortunate bird might have slept at his lookout post and not given warning of the approach of some enemy.

One October the crows didn't come back. And they never have returned. But once after they had ceased to come here, I saw them far, far up in the sky like motes, forming a long straight road of life flying westward. It was a narrow road perhaps fifteen or twenty crows wide but it stretched as far as I could see from horizon to horizon. There, I suppose, went our crows off to some other farm than ours, and I have always missed them.

Another time my sister and I were driving north from a vacation at Beaufort in South Carolina when we turned aside to visit Lake Mattamuskeet in North Carolina, which had lately been made into a refuge (with some limited hunting) by flooding acres and acres of former asparagus lands. A concrete powerhouse with a high chimney stack, standing beside a sluiceway, had been made into a rest house, I think very recently, and while it had a certain modern beauty, a starker place I have never seen. We were shown to our concrete cells, and then went out to the lake in the late afternoon. Flocks of duck and of Canada geese came wheeling in, and later a smaller flock of swans. And it was the cries of the swans that echoed through our dreams and sounded like clarions whenever we awoke in the darkness.

Another year Henry and I had been going a great deal to Quebec while he was writing his book on the St. Lawrence, and friends there had told us of the excitement they felt when the snow geese flew over the roofs of the city by night on their spring and fall way to their feeding grounds farther down the river.

"We'll telegraph you," they promised, and one autumn day a message arrived:

"The snow geese are at Cap Tourment."

Immediately we packed our suitcases and started our drive north. It was early October and beyond Quebec the birch-covered mountains stood clothed in solid gold-leaf. Where the highway, rising inland, left the St. Lawrence, we followed a narrow road close to the water, and passing a large farm and its cows, came to low-lying land at a great blue turn of the river. On the land side rose the cliff of Cap Tourment, over which hung a waterfall whose sound, varied and dispersed, was taken up and magnified by a continual creaking and honking. The green meadows were covered with the geese, white, close-set, like foam caught in the grasses when a tide goes out, or perhaps like banks of snow beginning to soften in the spring. Above them flew other flocks of geese, perhaps a dozen or a hundred or five hundred together, some flying low, some high up in the air, circling over the meadows or the blue river, flying slowly against the cold wind, or swiftly with it. In spite of black wing-tips, they were apparently pure white as the sun struck them, and dark as they turned, each group and wheeling squadron continually honking as it flew, continually answered by the multitude below, in one wild lovely monotonous clangor like nothing we have ever heard, nor could hear, unless forty thousand geese were resting and feeding on the meadows of the St. Lawrence.

That glimpse was as near as we have ever come to seeing the North America which Audubon knew, and it was near enough for its memory to remain with us for the rest of our lives.

Minister's Child

I HAVE a very charming friend who has gardenias every winter from a great plant slipped long ago from the first gardenia her first beau gave her to wear to her first dance. There must be an inheritance of gaiety, prettiness, and lightness of touch in the family, for one day she told me a story of her grandmother, whom I am sure she is just like.

As a girl, Grandmother lived in a small Maine town where her father was the minister. It was early spring—not mud-time, but the time when the maples are in blossom and the apples are in bud. The village girls were in a great state of excitement because a young man of the place had returned for a visit to his parents after some years spent in the Sandwich Islands, or perhaps they were already called the Hawaiian Islands. He was said to have made a fortune. He was said to be thrillingly handsome. And then he was such a romantic figure! Few people had seen him yet, but it was known that he would be at church, and it was spring, and the young girls were in a frenzy, choosing their dresses and bonnets.

The sixteen-year-old daughter of the minister was as excited as anyone. I imagine more excited, but in an airy, merry fashion. And then her father spoiled it all by saying that she could not attend the morning service. She must stay at home and be nurse to the younger children. She was left there in her old housedress with bad little brothers and sisters, while all the other girls in town went by in their prettiest dresses looking like so many cats who have been lapping cream. She heard the church bells ringing across the new grass, and saw the lazy Sunday curls of smoke from the chimneys, and perhaps later she could even hear the sound of hymns slanting out from the open windows of the church. There the girls were, all singing their loudest, hoping to catch the eye of the young man, coquetting under their bonnet brims, or tilting their wicked little chins as though their thoughts were only on heaven; and here she was, indoors, in her old dress, wiping Betsy's nose and telling Asa not to eat the buttons from the sewing basket!

The long service came at last to its end, and at the church door a bevy of townsfolk surrounded the wanderer, half neighbor, half stranger after these years of absence. Probably he saw a ring of pretty faces, heard a whole chorus of bird voices, was pierced by a battery of eyes peeping at him through their lashes.

And then he walked home under the spring-red maples with his papa and mamma, and as he passed the minister's house there was a stir at an open window and between the white curtains a little figure appeared. Although she was going nowhere she had on the choicest of bonnets, and lace mitts were on the hands parting the curtains, and the face that looked out was smiling above the prettiest of dresses.

"Hello, John Edwards!" the vision called. "Won't you marry me?"

His name was not John Edwards. But otherwise the story is true. And he married her.

The Olivers

THE OLIVERS' KITCHEN is usually filled with people, just as the spaces between the parallel barn and shed and kitchen doors are likely to be filled with cats and their kittens. The house hasn't been painted for years and has the silvery moth-wing look which I am very fond of. The two great elms darkening the seldom-used front door are not marriage trees as I supposed, but rather birthday trees, and were planted for old Mr. Oliver's two sisters, who are still alive and although old themselves drive their car occasionally down the East Neck Road for a visit. "How fast trees grow in Maine!" as someone said to me only yesterday. "People talk about growth in the tropics, but these short Maine summers force the trees just as fast."

Certainly to look at the elms intertwining their branches high above the roofs of the buildings you would say that they had stood there for more than a hundred years. Well, after all, they have been there a long time.

We climb two steep steps and rap at the screen door which is often "buttoned," as people say in these parts, to keep it from blowing open in the wind. The kitchen is almost square, and its remarkable feature is its floor with narrow boards laid in concentric squares about a single small square of black-cherry wood at its very center. There have never been rugs or linoleum on the floor; a thousand scrubbings have worn it smooth and soft-grained. The window over the sink looks out across the Hathe and its sluggish stream. As fall comes on, Mrs. Oliver reports the deer, fox, and moose that she sees from this window; but at other times of the year she can tell you with accuracy every car and person who has passed along the road and the hour at which they went by, a faculty which is a great help to us when we are trying to trace who it was who came to call when we were out, or what light truck drove by late in the evening, turned about, and drove away without stopping.

Mrs. Oliver is a very handsome, straight-standing woman, a good deal younger than Mr. Oliver, with his drooping white mustache and his eyes so blue and humorous in his tanned face.

Barbara, before she married Irving, the Olivers' only son, was in our household for several years, so she seems part of the family, with her rosy face and easy laugh. She is almost always in the kitchen with Mrs. Oliver and the two little boys, one still a baby. Irving is home, not working at the shipyards as he has done for nearly two years. Two of his ribs are mending after a fall from a scaffolding, and here is one of those curious coincidences which seem to occur more often in the country than in the city. Irving broke his ribs a year to a day from the time that his father fell off the hayrack last summer and broke his. There was a woman hereabouts who was twice married, and each of her husbands was blinded in one eye by an accident with barbed wire. We used to see her, and she had a sad puzzled look as though she couldn't understand how such an unusual thing could have happened twice over to her.

But here strangeness is more accepted than among people who constantly read other men's ideas and are more closely gripped in the world of machinery. When Henry tells about his dream of a chimney fire and of meeting Mrs. Simmons in a car with some of her family, all in a great state of unsettledness, and about how he told Annie and me of his dream twenty-four hours before the Simmons house actually caught fire at the chimney and burned into the cellar—no one is at all surprised, nor offers the slightest rationalized explanation. Here the isolated families, fighting their separate fights against Fate and the encroaching wilderness, are aware of curious recurrences and accept them.

Although work is hard on the Oliver farm with Mr. Oliver growing old, and Mrs. Oliver not very strong, and Irving away most of the day, and the chicken yard to be attended to and the eggs to be gathered, weighed, and packed, and the little boys to be taken care of, the Oliver kitchen is a very jolly place. The whole family dearly loves a joke, and loves to laugh and to sing. Mr. Oliver tells us sometimes of the old days, of his grandfather who about 1800 brought his wife into the wilderness on horseback and built a log cabin between the two old apple trees which still look over the Hathe, growing above an old well, covered with a great stone. Or he will tell of early days at the sawmill at the head of the bay where fifty teams of oxen would come in a row hauling lumber down the ice, or of the well he climbed down into as a boy, from which he could see a star at midday, or of the raccoon his mother baked, which tasted so good until he knew what it was.

"Why is the place where the water drains into the Hathe called Witch Bridge?" I asked one day. "Was there a witch?"

Mr. Oliver's face lighted up reminiscently.

"Well, when we all were children we used to stay up at the end of the road pretty late. Wouldn't get home until after dark. Mother used to tell us to come home, but you know how children are. So one evening we were coming along, late as usual. You know it's pretty lonely in that stretch with the bushes growing close on one side of the road and the Hathe stretching out on the other. It was almost dark, just bright enough to see things still, when all of a sudden something big and white came out of the bushes waving its arms at us. The hair rose right up on our heads, and we ran home in a hurry, I tell you. Mother wasn't in, but she came in soon after with her sewing bag over her arm. Said she'd been up at my aunt's across the road. We children didn't stop to put two and two together; we had so much to tell her about the witch who had chased us. She just nodded and nodded and said, 'Dear me,' and 'Gracious.' She didn't even tell us we'd better never go on that road again in the dark. But you can bet we were home for meals on time after that. It was years before any of us would cross Witch Bridge after the sun had gone down.

"My mother was a wonderful woman," he added. "When she died we gave up cooking in the open fireplace. We bricked it up just as it was, with the andirons and the crane and the big hanging pot all in their places. They must be there to this day, in case anyone ever wants to use them again."

Lambs

ONE JUNE we felt that we should have more animal life on the farm, so we called on Hudson Vannah and borrowed a lamb from his flock to keep for the summer. I had memories of a black lamb which I had once seen in a Nova Scotian village, with a red bow on its neck, following its little-girl mistress to the post office like an animated verse from a school reader. Our elder daughter, Meg, who from earliest childhood has been the wild-strawberry picker among us, was at camp, but Kate was not at camp, and now should have a lamb. I insisted on a ewe, which could be returned without fear of the autumn butchering (it is pronounced "bootchering" with us). Unfortunately all the lambs had been born rather early that year. The lamb which was finally forced into the back of our car seemed rather large and strong to me, but Kate greeted her with enthusiasm at our door and named her Blanche, with a sweeping Eve-like assurance.

All summer Blanche was a part of the farm life, but such a part! She was stupid, dull, and greedy. She felt no impulse to play or to follow her little-girl mistress or anyone else anywhere. I spent hours taking ticks from her fleece and dropping them into a tomato can filled with kerosene, but though Blanche throve amazingly she showed neither character nor affection. The only place one could be sure to find her was at the tea table under the apple trees at four o'clock in the afternoon; and there she baaed, nagging persistently, ready to eat everything she was given with small sidewise twists of her narrow jaw. And one afternoon, when three unknown ladies came to interview Henry and the tray arrived while we were all in the herb garden, Blanche did not wait to be given her treat but reached up and took it for herself—not only her share, but everybody else's as well.

I had once imagined that Blanche's future fate would be a matter of great concern to me; but such wasn't the case. When she was finally returned I didn't care what might happen to her; I forgot all my plans for mittens and socks to be knitted from her wool. In fact Blanche was not *simpatica*. It was with Kate, then about five, that my real sympathy lay when one dull afternoon I saw that enterprising little-girl mistress chasing her pet around the corner of the house with a broom.

"Kate!" I cried in hypocritical reproof. "Why in the world are you hitting Blanche?"

Kate looked me in the eye.

"I'm trying to make her *do* something, Mother!"

I'm sure a run would have done Blanche good, but I played the mother's monotonous part and stopped the poor attempt at sport.

The pair of lambs that Mrs. Rollins once told us about were very different. They had been raised on the bottle, never having known a mother, and were very fat. But the little male insisted upon running with the hounds. The first time, it went with them only a little way into the woods and came back by itself; the second time, it went clear across the Neck and someone "hitched" it. Mrs. Rollins's father could hear it bleating, and the hounds led him straight to the right farm when he drove off to find the runaway. The lamb did the same thing another two or three times, and finally old Mr. Hall decided he would have to sell it, much as he hated to. It was such a lively creature, but it made too much trouble. A lamb ought to behave like a lamb and not like a hound dog.

Sailor's Return

COMMUNITY LIVING, like soil, lies layer upon layer. You only know one surface at a time; with every day some sense of the other buried surfaces comes in a chance word here and a chance word there. For instance, until a week or so ago I never knew that old Mr. Oliver's father had ever left the gray farmhouse where he was born and died.

We happened to be talking of the barn across the road which belongs to the other branch of the Oliver family. The original holding has been divided into shapes of land as unexpected as pieces in a jigsaw puzzle, yet all of course with a meaning—each family has its lake front, its hay land, its garden land, its pasture and its wood lots; but they of necessity fall so strangely that the Oliver house on the knoll overlooking the end of the pond is surrounded by land on both sides belonging to the Olivers on the road below them, and its only connection with the main road is a strip of soil scarcely wide enough to carry the lane. At first glance, it would be hard to tell who owned the barn. Although it is not his, Father Oliver knew its history very well.

"That barn?" he repeated, turning his blue eyes upon it, eyes which seem especially blue in his tanned face. "That was built in 1852. Often heard my father say that the year they built that barn the field was planted to yellow corn far as the eye could see. He wasn't home winters those days. Went as a cook with a lumber crew to Virginia. Man named Sam Haines used to build boats at Scotty. Winters, he'd fit out a schooner; take his own food, with molasses for sweetening; put in his own yoke of oxen and a little hay; take a crew of loggers and sail for Virginia. My father went along as cook. All winter the loggers would cut timber and load the schooner, and in the spring Sam would load the oxen and crew—there wouldn't be much hay, or food, or sweetening left by that time—and sail north for a summer of ship-building with the timbers he'd got in Virginia. My father was away six or seven winters with Sam."

Recently in the little Maine Museum at Searsport we saw pictures of vessels which were even built in the South by Searsport ship-builders with Searsport capital. They were registered as hailing from Searsport, although one of them sailed for seventeen years and was finally lost at sea without ever having touched at her official home port.

The people of the coast in those days were enterprising and imaginative. They sought what they wanted, when they didn't have it at home, and I have wondered that there were no more traces of the sea on our road, but I was too hasty in coming to that conclusion. Only the other day Henry stopped the car before Miss Vannah's house. As we drove up she was standing looking down at her roses, which grow in great blankets ten or fifteen feet long on her lawn, true beds of roses red with bloom. Miss Vannah is nearly eighty years old, but she lives alone at the edge of the woods, next to her nephew's farm. One still sees her in a fresh print dress mending the road in front of her cottage, bringing small stones and baskets of earth to fill in the ruts. She welcomed us kindly and brought us in to the screened porch, and a moment later she came out of the house with an envelope.

"My cousin's daughter sent this to me when her mother died at ninety a little while ago. I have my own copy of it somewhere, but I don't know where it is. You are the only people I could think of who would be interested." (She had written Henry a postcard of which he hadn't spoken, waiting for the right moment.)

Carefully she unfolded a newspaper which had been printed in Waldoboro in 1872. As she talked my eye fell on notices of smallpox cases in the various towns, and of the beginning of the season for using the river for drays and sleighs; and I smiled at one advertisement: "E. T. Gay offers better tobacco than Major Clark ever thought of selling at the depot." The Gay store still dominates the village, although it has passed out of the family's hands.

But it was not for local items that Miss Vannah had saved the newspaper. Two columns on one page were taken up by an obituary which the editor himself had written for Captain Zina Vannah.

"He was Father's younger brother," Miss Vannah said. "I remember that night well. I was six years old at the time." And she asked Henry to read the account aloud to us.

You must think of us sitting in the coolness and semidarkness of the screened-in porch with the sun and the roses and the bees and the woods outside, and the pug dog waiting in the car, drawn half off the narrow dirt road. Henry has the most beautiful reading voice I have ever heard. He read very simply the somewhat flowery phrases of the young editor who had been Zina Vannah's friend. I say "flowery," and yet perhaps the writing had a kind of truth about it which would be missed today.

The account began with a description of the day after Christmas, and of gentlemen returning to the warmth and welcome of their own firesides. It dwelt on the well-being and close cheer of the families at that season, when all was secure, while outside the storm was rising and the snow dashed against the window panes and far away, off Cape Cod, three gallant ships were being done to death in the icy breakers. The largest of these was the *Peruvian,* an East Indiaman of twelve hundred tons, returning after a year in the East Indies. She had been sighted on the morning of December 26th, under full sail, entering Massachusetts Bay, apparently safe after her long journey. Then came the blizzard, and all the rest was lost in the blinding snow. At first, only one thing came to the beach unbroken from the *Peruvian,* and that was the ship's clock, stopped at a little after four—people thought in the afternoon. Later the bodies began to come in.

Then followed a short account of the captain's life. At fourteen he had served on the *Niobe* of Waldoboro, from whose decks he had seen a brother washed into the sea and drowned. He had risen rapidly in a series of vessels, including at least one from Damariscotta, and had recently been made captain of the *Peruvian,* which he had sailed to the great satisfaction of the owners.

"I think he was only twenty-eight," added Miss Vannah. "My father went right down to the Cape when the news came. He hired divers. The wreck lay only half a mile off land, in plain sight. But not one man came ashore alive. My father brought Uncle Zina's body here to be buried."

"The wreck was probably at Peaked Hill Bars," said Henry. "I think I remember hearing of the *Peruvian.*"

"Yes, that was the place," Miss Vannah agreed eagerly. "I thought you might be interested."

On the way home we stopped to see Captain Zina's grave in the group under four elms overlooking, as does everything else on that beautiful farm, the lake and Loon Island and the hills beyond. There, beneath a headstone showing a ship under full sail, lies the captain in the earth of the family farm, within sound of the passing horses and buggy wheels, and now of the cars and trucks and tractors, within sound of the unchanging crowing of the cocks and the lowing of the milch cows and the bleating of the sheep which always gives this farm an air of classic beauty. Sometimes a sea gull goes by overhead, crying harshly into the wind. Perhaps it was that cry which came to him as a young boy pitching hay in these fields, and made him restless for the sea beyond the headlands. At all events, he went, and now he has returned.

Decoration Day

TOWARDS the end of May the families in this part of the country begin to think about their graveyards. You will come upon cars parked by the side of country roads while a whole household uproots bushes, scythes the weeds, and cuts the grass in farm burial plots. Then a tilted headstone is righted, the boulder walls straightened, and the jars brought from the pantry ready for flowers.

One Decoration Day stands out in my mind because of its simple sweetness. We began by carrying lilacs up to the burial ground in our own hayfield, and Henry read a Psalm as we stood by its white picket fence, looking in at the myrtle growing over the graves of those strangers who had worked these fields and cooked and washed in the low farmhouse before ever we came to it. To them we owe all the labor of clearing the land, of planting the old high-top apples by the door, and of building well the house and shed and barn. Their roses bloom still; the clump of lilacs from which I broke the brittle twigs was planted to please some farm woman here; we find their mints and mallows. Although we are no kin of theirs, we share their inheritance and are bound to them by the tie of fields and woods.

As we drove to town, we passed a pasture where two women and a group of children were scattered, carrying lilacs and wild-cherry branches up a hill towards a farm burying ground. Later we came upon a man and his daughter walking along the side of the road with a few sprays of flowers in their hands, and next we passed an old horse and buggy with wilted wild flowers in the shadow of the seat. It was a quiet procession of the living to the houses of the dead.

"What are all those little churches?" Meg once asked me when she was little, as we passed a graveyard, and on Decoration Day each gravestone is indeed an altar where prayers are said. New flags fly on the graves of soldiers, and flowers stand at the foot of most of the stones.

On this particular day, we arrived at Damariscotta in time for the official Memorial Day procession, led by the Legion band in dark tunics and bright yellow helmets and yellow trousers. They reminded us of figures in a Chippendale wallpaper, a surprisingly charming effect. After them followed the colors and some Legionnaires and two cars filled with veterans, very old men with the blue blank look of their years, and then came the school children, the girls looking a little cold in their white dresses, their small flags whipping in the misty breeze.

At the bridge between the two towns the procession halted, and the Scottish minister standing in the center of the bridge read a Psalm and prayed; and then the Legion commander walked forward and threw a bouquet of flowers into the river beneath. The cold green tide was pouring out towards the sea and carried the flowers with it as a memorial to the sailors who had died in the war. Three ragged volleys of shots rang out, frightening the sea gulls, and the bugle played Taps and a ghostly bugle answered from far away, as though the dead replied to the voice of the living.

We stood watching the bright speck of color which was the bouquet until it slowly sank in an eddy and was gone—still drifting seaward, no doubt. Perhaps the ghosts of the drowned had taken it to themselves. Perhaps they knew nothing about it, but for the living the broad green river was touched with a holiness as it ran, silently and strongly, between its shores of granite, pine, and hayfield.

Our Friend and Gardener

IN 1941 LAWRENCE, our hired man at the farm, left us to join the army. He was twenty-five years old and must have felt a vague desire to see something of the world; and at that time the threat of war hung ever present along the horizon, and the air was uneasy with the sense of coming storm. He was a private in the first regular army some months before Pearl Harbor, and his younger brother Ellis took his place with us at the farm. Sometimes Lawrence came to see us on furlough and stayed for dinner or spent the night. He looked well and seemed satisfied: the army treated you fine—good food—the boys were good fellows.

His letters dealt more with the farm and with us than with himself. This was to be more apparent when he went overseas and landed at Casablanca. The impact of North Africa, of fighting, of the entire Arab civilization could scarcely succeed in wrenching a remark from him. It was our healths after which he politely inquired, and memories of scything in the orchard or swimming in Deep Cove which were invoked. Once he wrote that he had picked oranges from the trees, but that they were sour.

His regiment marched through Sicily, as support troops. He told us that the people brought grapes to the side of the road; otherwise his letters said little save that he wished he were at the farm again. About this time he found a charming phrase with which to close: "Your friend and gardener."

England he liked. We heard rumors of an English girl. He was at the landing on the Normandy beaches, and fought through Normandy, but all he told us was that the climate was much like England; nor did he mention the Distinguished Service

Cross which came to join the Silver Star he had won in Africa. He was at Aachen and saw it pulverized from the air. He fought across Germany. This we might infer from a word of praise which he gave to the farms. In those years of fighting he never uttered any complaint. It was difficult to know how much he had seen or felt.

When word came in the papers that the men with more than eighty-five points were to be mustered out, we felt sure that we should soon see Lawrence. He had no dependents, it is true, but we knew that he had been in six major battles and had won at least two decorations. Would he be willing to come back to the farm, we wondered. Annie, our housekeeper, had been forced by age to retire; our girls were away and the house seemed very quiet. We could get no one to mow the tall grass that grew up to the sills, giving the neat buildings an unkempt look. Sometimes a discouragement came upon us. Two years earlier we had for the first time found no one to cut the hay; the barn roof was going, and we feared that the entire building might be lost, its roof falling through to the floor in great pieces of old boards and shingles, bending over fallen beams like heavy wrapping paper. Alas, how many such barns have we seen on the back roads! We could find no one to renew the rotting entrance to the kitchen door. The plumber had turned iceman and now ran a woodyard.

Although after many efforts Henry succeeded in having the barn reshingled and the hay cut, the farm had an uncared-for look again this summer. Then came the Fourth of July, and we heard that Lawrence was back at his father's. A week later he appeared at the door.

Lawrence! The years rolled back. Nearly five years have gone by, but he looks no older. Brown, sandy-haired, brawny, and smiling, his glance is as untroubled as ever. What terrible memories have become part of his being? He does not speak of them. In open blue shirt, light-blue cotton trousers, and old shoes, he sits at ease by the kitchen table with its red cloth and talks while we gather about exclaiming and asking questions. How lucky that he came on Friday when Marion helps us and brings a roasted chicken! We can still celebrate, and there are new peas, and the old-fashioned rose by the back door is in full bloom. The pug dog seems to recognize him and sits watching him as do the rest of us.

Lawrence, old-timer, how is everything?

There is a rumor of a girl in Massachusetts and of a job in a war factory there, but he does not talk of them. He does not believe in universal military training. "Us boys all say eight weeks' training is better than a year's. A fellow gets stale doing things over and over again. It's in battle you learn." Now he mentions Africa, and casually says: "Once they cut us off, and we were three days without food. And water. That was worse." "We gave them a good chance at Aachen. A day to sign in, and then the planes circled for fifteen minutes before they began to drop their bombs." "We could see the Eiffel Tower from where we were stationed for a while, but I only went to Paris once." "No, I never was seasick though lots of the boys was. I liked the sea." "I'd tell any son of mine never to enlist unless he had to. The places I've seen don't make up for being in battle. Of two hundred and fifty of us in our company who went over together, only thirty-five came back. I had a hundred and thirty-two points, and I didn't fall for any re-enlisting pep talk. The officer says to us when we went to muster out, 'You remember civilian life is hard.' 'Yes, sir,' I says to him. 'And did you ever happen to notice that life at the front is hard, too?' "

Lawrence has more to say than he had five years ago. He has been places, he has seen things, he has lived through much, and has twice been decorated for courage. He has opinions, and he has questions. That vague figure "some white-collar fellow" appears in his talk, like the villain of the piece; the mistakes, the schemings are his.

But he doesn't want to talk for long. He has seen the grass brushing against the red clapboards of the house. He goes out to the barn and takes down the crooked scythe, and soon we see him straddled and at ease, his arms swinging regularly, the grass whispering as it falls at his feet. For two days and a half he works untiringly, raking the heavy hay and carrying it away in the familiar wheelbarrow; he works with the sickle, too, and the long shears. We know that he does not like to be interrupted or disturbed. This is his art. The old, not-very-sharp lawn mower begins to rattle and chirr like a grasshopper. Its song is short too, like a grasshopper's leap, for it comes to a jolting halt at a tuft of grass, and often needs to have the dried grasses cut away from the edges of its blades, where they twist themselves into a stubborn knot.

Carefully the rough lawn is cut; again the house stands on its terrace flanked by the old apple trees; again the herb garden, sheltered in the ell of the house, is cut clear. Before dinner Lawrence runs down to the lake for a swim. Luckily a few days ago we had a gift of meat, and we have something filling to give him after his work.

So for a week he is to remain with us, helping Henry with the outdoor chores which have been piling up. He slips back into the old pattern so naturally. He suits the fields, and the fields suit him. Perhaps he will grow tired of a city and of machinery and come back here with a wife and find an empty farm as his brothers have done and start off for himself the unending but varied tasks of a small Maine farmer. Whatever he does will be well and solidly done, with little said about it.

I remember in one of his letters a mention of the African fight in which he won the Silver Star (he did not mention the star). Surely Maine understatement could scarcely go further. In the midst of his usual detailed inquiries about us and the farm appeared a single casual sentence:

"We have just come through a long, hot, and tiresome battle."

Tiresome! Well, no doubt it was.

The Writing on the Wall

NO ONE hates names, dates, and addresses scribbled on old walls and in empty broken-in-upon houses more than I; but there is another kind of inscription, written from some deep emotion and left on plaster or glass, which seems to carry with it the very touch of the generation and the moment of its writing. I should like to see a collection of such immediate messages, perhaps from all parts of the world, but our own country is surely rich enough.

I remember the beautiful Spanish writing scratched with a dagger in the sandstone of Inscription Rock in the midst of the bare mesas of New Mexico, carved some weary evening while Spanish soldiers lounged about a campfire under that narrow waterfall which has made its own cavern in the rock. There is a house in New Castle, Delaware, on whose chamber window a lover wrote with a diamond a poem calling upon angels to guard the pure sleep of his beloved. Washington himself stood at the hearth when the couple were later married. Then I have read on a New England attic beam the outcry of a child, "June 3, 1862 today Mother drowned all of Blacky's kittens," written at about the time that a Confederate soldier scrawled an angry message on the plaster of a great house in Arkansas which had been headquarters for the Southerners.

"We're leaving but we'll be back, you damned Yankees," I think were the words which the unknown man wrote with a piece of charcoal. He never came back; but his defiance still stands, left here in that wallpapered room, for who could cover that burning bitterness with paper roses or neat lattices?

Still the graffito I like best is calm and benign, a message written on the plaster above the landing of the cellar stairs in a Waldoboro house which stands on a high series of terraces shadowed by elms overlooking the fields and the stream below. The man who built the house was a great shipowner and a great gentleman. We have several of his old books bound in calfskin, of which my favorite is a Horace in Latin, much handled and much loved. Surely he wrote with a classical mellowness when he stood that day on the landing of his new home and gave it his final blessing:

I. G. Reed
built this House 1814–1816
Inhabited it April 1816
He wishes health, prosperity
and contented minds to all his
successors

Voyagers

WHENEVER we walk down the hayfields to the opening in the alders by the lake, right the canoe and carry it half-dragging over the maple's bared roots to the shallows, and there launch it with our picnic basket in the shade of the pointed bow, I feel a sense of excitement. Most of our canoeing is done in September and October and on warm days in November. We slip away from the reflection of our trees, sometimes to the islands, sometimes to the clear-cut coves of the west shore with their rocks and pines, sometimes to the overgrown coves of the east shore with their lilies floating among round flat leaves, or their lost lagoons of reeds, turned golden, from which the ducks fly up with a whistling of wings.

That country sense of excitement, of expecting to meet the unexpected, goes with us even when nothing unusual happens. Very small things are enough to give us that start of pleasure: an eagle rising from a rock with his white tail low over the water, like some great flying rabbit; a wedge of wild geese overhead continually changing their formation, save for the leader at the point of the arrow; loons calling to us in their wild shaken notes, and sometimes running along the surface of the water with a plashing and splashing most beautiful to hear and most joyous to see. Small birds fly in and out of the thickets along the shore, at this time of the year a band of color, beaded by the scarlet berries of the black alder. Occasionally we stop to watch the ribbon of young alewives rippling along the shallows, nearly a foot in width and hundreds of feet long. In the clear reflections of rocks we have watched the black bass lie. And some day, we are very sure that we shall come upon a moose feeding in the shallows.

Damariscotta is a lake with no history of which we have ever heard. Its only fleets have been the lumber rafts of fifty years ago sailing in the spring to the sawmills. Through the clear water nearer the shore we can sometimes see logs lying, mavericks from the floating herds which once traveled these bays. Every position brings us to a new perspective, of fields and farms which in Indian Summer seem Arcadian in their beauty rising above the water, or of marshes and pine-grave headlands, in a landscape apparently so untouched by man that we feel like the first-comers peering out upon the austere loveliness of an innocent and unpeopled region.

Last week, as we were nearing home waters, Henry exclaimed, "See ahead of us."

I looked up and saw something which seemed like a large snapping turtle swimming towards the land. The lozenge-shaped head was raised above the surface, and what I took to be the shell was nearly a foot long. We were facing into the sun at the time and could distinguish little beyond a rapid and resolute motion heading towards the bank.

When the canoe drew up beside the swimmer, however, we found that our turtle was a gray squirrel. What a swimmer the creature was! He flowed along the water as though he had a dozen legs. His back and the top of his long tail were perfectly dry, and so was the head held above the surface. Henry said, "He looks tired, like an exhausted man." Certainly he eyed us uneasily, but as we paddled beside him he refused to deflect his course. There was no pitiful dodging or shifting. He swam steadily on, only his anguished eye admitting our presence. At a boulder, he emerged nimbly enough; but, leaping to the shore, he miscalculated the weight of his wet body and fell into the shallows again, scrambling out in a jiffy. We glanced back at the eastern shore, nearly a mile away. Was he part of that strange migration of squirrels, red and gray, which swim westward across the great rivers of the East when a hard winter lies ahead? No one to whom we spoke had ever seen a swimming squirrel; but sometimes in the fall the papers report them.

If one gray squirrel made a rather touching pioneer (go west, young squirrel, go west!) there were stranger and more ethereal travelers on the move yesterday. It was the first mild day we have had for a month, and the southeast breeze was so slight that it never brushed the water or stirred a leaf in the dry and brilliant thickets. As we came into our own cove we became aware that we were by no means alone in our traveling. The sunny air was crossed by glints and slivers of light, some floating parallel to the water, four or five feet in the air, a few in fine half-circles, and more at spearlike angles, advancing with one end high in the air, and the other nearly or quite touching the still surface. They were the threads by which the young spiders travel seeking adventure in the world, colonizing new lands. The almost imperceptible breeze carried the threads at a surprising speed.

We pursued several, where the spider hung close to the water, now touching it and sailing on like a little boat leaving a V-shaped ripple behind him, now swinging clear for another ten feet, only to return to the lake and speed on once more with a sail five feet long and narrow as gossamer. The tension of the surface did not betray the voyagers. Their pale legs and bodies glided over the mirrorlike substance of the pond, as though it were a solid. As far as we could see, they did not run upon it, but were carried, each by his thread, on and on towards the shore.

Certainly many must have been lost; but more appeared to be reaching the land. Where was the launching of that almost invisible fleet, and whose the will which decided that the day and moment were propitious and ordered the lines cast off, and the colony to start forth for an unseen land beyond the waters?

Sound and Clever

FOR SEVERAL YEARS Irving at the farm down the road has been working at Waldoboro, helping to build wooden ships, returning to that old art—or should one call it craft?—which once built up the town, and paid for the big square houses where lived the captains and owners of the shipyards, and added U.S. CUSTOM HOUSE to the sign over the door of the post office. It has become again a pleasure to look from the shell-heaps of the old button factory, across the green tidal headwaters of the river to the shipyards under the trees on the other side. When we were last there, two or three hulls lay in their cradles with men moving about them, and the air was busy with the sounds of hammers and saws. Two of the vessels were roofed over in casual sheds; another lay in the river, already launched but awaiting the final touches.

In summer the scene was a pretty one, and well suited to the town and its history, and Irving, who has the farmer's knack of turning his hand to many things, enjoyed the work. But in winter it was another story: the freezing winds blew into the open faces of the sheds, and men's hands were numb with cold, and coughing twisted at their chests. Sometimes the roads were impassable—once or twice Irving's car was stuck in a snowdrift; nor did eight hours on the windy scaffoldings finish his work, for there was always more to be done on the farm in the darkness of the short winter days, although his father and Barbara loyally took over all they could of the chores in the chicken yards and the barn.

Then, one fall, the yards began to lay off men, as the government orders for wooden ships had stopped and there were only occasional fishing schooners to be built. Irving decided not to wait to be fired; he left work and returned to the farm. Perhaps he would miss the talk of other men as they worked; perhaps he might sometimes recall the pride with which ship-builders see a good vessel launched. But though the work on a farm is an unending, never-finished succession of duties, one pulling at a man's sleeve before he has finished with another, Irving was glad to be back in his own place and master of his own decisions and time.

"Irving has a nice little nest egg in the bank," Barbara told us. There has been no wartime spending at the Oliver farm; everything has gone on quietly in its accustomed groove as in the old days. With Malcolm only five and John not yet two, they have had an eye to the future in the gray house under the big elm trees.

So I was surprised when Barbara, arriving once more to help with supper, said: "Irving bought a pair of horses today. He says he'd rather have them than a tractor. They're beauties, white with gray dapples. Came from up at the head of the pond."

It is a long time since anyone on our road has had a pair of horses. One elderly horse sometimes languishes, usually unseen and unsuspected, in the depths of a barn, to come out almost to its own surprise and assist with the haying or in hauling a wagonload of wood. I remember that our friend Jake Day once spoke of such a horse as "having taken the veil." The Olivers themselves have had a good old creature, poor Rosy, with her bony head gray with age, and a preternaturally long tail and a great mane matted far down on her shoulders. Since Rosy's predecessor was bogged in the quicksands of the Hathe, and had to be shot after being pulled out, only the cows have been allowed to follow the interlaced pasture paths above the marsh, and we have scarcely a bowing acquaintance with Rosy.

But of course we were eager to see the new horses, which were young, big, and matched. They belonged to a man who that summer was pulling a hayrack back to the barn behind his tractor. His father was standing on the load. Some obstruction made the tractor give a jerk which was transmitted to the rack with double force, and the older man was thrown from the hay and broke his neck. His son was left heavy-hearted, with all the work to do, and twelve cows to milk. The team had to be given up.

So there they stood in the Oliver barn. When we drove Barbara home, only Mrs. Oliver was in the kitchen.

"The others are all in the barn," she said, and we went out through the shed to join them. The scene had the quality which we associate with the Dutch painters, of darkness faintly yellowed by candlelight. Here the glow came from a lantern in the passage behind the tie-up, and in the vague radiance we could see the figures of three generations of Olivers and of a neighbor from the next farm.

"Come in and see the white elephants," Irving called, opening the door into the two horse stalls and holding up the lantern. There, side by side, stood vast twin figures; dappled flanks rose up to within eight inches of the low roof; strong frames filled the spaces almost from side wall to side wall. As we stood gazing, one quiet dappled head turned to look at us, and then turned back again.

"Daddy, I'll have to get a ladder to climb one of those," said Malcolm, and we all laughed.

"Where is Rosy?" I asked.

Rosy was in a cow stall. She was going soon to another farm in exchange for a heifer. The man meant to keep her at least for the winter to get out some wood from his wood lot. And then—— Well, that's the way things go. This was the hour of the big team, the young team, the beauties.

But I felt a kind of sadness in them too, despite all the rejoicing which surrounded them, and with which they were welcomed. For a few days they must mourn for their old barn, their old fields, their former master. Then they would adjust themselves to the change. The important thing to them was that they had not been separated. They were still to go on working side by side as they had done since they were first broken into harness and had left the untroubled freedom of their colthood.

Irving patted a dappled side.

"I tell him he's as fond of his big boys as he is of his little boys," said Barbara, jokingly, for Irving is a devoted father.

"I'm pretty fond of them, and that's a fact," said Irving. He had earned them by many hours of ship-building, by many, many risings before the first crack of winter light. Now their presence dignified the farm and all the work in which they were to share.

"I never saw more biddable creatures," Irving said as he closed the door of the stalls for the night. "The only trouble we had with them was just for a minute. Major was taken out of the truck first and put in his stall. Prince couldn't see him and thought he'd lost him. You ought to have heard him whinny, and jump about in the truck! He was crazy till he saw Major again, and then he was just as quiet as he is now. They're a real good team, sound and clever."

"I hope so," said Mr. Oliver a little doubtfully. "A lot can happen to a horse won't happen to a tractor."

Something Cool

THERE LIVED many years ago in a neighboring town a solitary woman who, they say, "wrote." No one seems to have the least idea what she wrote, but the memory of desk, ink, and pen clings to her story. As she got on in years she made herself a shroud, to have on hand for her burial if she should sometime be taken suddenly ill.

Not long after the shroud was finished and folded away in a lower bureau drawer, there came a spell of very hot weather. I imagine that the clothes of the period were tight and very uncomfortable in the heat. It occurred to the lady that the shroud would be loose and easy to wear in the house during the hot spell, and could be put to some use before it took on its grimmer duties.

The experiment was a complete success. The shroud, made like a loose white wrapper with wide sleeves and many pleats, proved very comfortable. She began to appear in her garden in it on hot afternoons. Finally she wore it when riding horseback. She discovered that there was nothing like a shroud for real comfort, and in summer she was rarely to be seen in anything else. She wore out shroud after shroud, and when she finally died, the neighbors had to make one for her, as there wasn't a shroud in the house fit to be worn.

Parson Bailey

AT THE TIME when the American colonies broke slowly and painfully, strand by strand, their ties with England, I wonder how many parsons preached revolt from the pulpit? It might be an interesting subject for a university Ph.D. My guess would be that the majority of them tried to rally their congregations to loyalty to the king. They were men of authority in their communities, pledged to an orderly way of life, and they could look back to an endless succession of prayers for the health of the king and of the royal family.

In Hingham, south of Boston, Ebenezer Gay was a stanch Loyalist, or Tory if you were on the other side of the fence. When the Committee of Safety came to search his house for weapons he placed his hand on the Bible. "Gentlemen, this is my only weapon," he said, speaking with that touch of ironic humor so characteristic of the man.

In these parts, the minister one hears of again and again is Parson Bailey. A man from Dresden had recently given us a pink Parson Bailey rose and a little white lilac, a scion of the one that had stood by Parson Bailey's house. On that fine day in late June, Frances and Kate and I thought we must find the source from which our new plants had originated.

We drove to Dresden and there saw many pale pink open-faced roses like our own. Then, crossing the bridge, we came to a narrow road turning left towards the Kennebec, and drove along it, hearing the bushes scrape on either side of the car as we passed. However, we persevered and presently came to a boulder with a tablet commemorating the site of the first Episcopal church, eighty feet to the southeast. Earth holds the traces of old workings for thousands of years and here it was only a question of less than two hundred, so without much trouble we found under the blueberry bushes a shallow ditch outlining the place where the church had stood. The ruins of the house were harder to come on. They were not marked as is usual with lost houses by any elm or clump of lilacs, and we had to work our way through pines, oaks, and fallen birches from one old clearing to another, until at last we again came to the ditchlike outline of a building, this time near a pile of stones in which someone had stuck a stick as a marker. Worked stone lay about, probably from the foundation, and we thought there was room for a garden before the land fell away to a branch of the river.

No smallest rose bush had survived, no white lilac in that wilderness, but ours may have been children of plants long ago taken to Dresden. Farther on along the road we came to a solitary house with a view cut through to the town, and pinks and Parson Bailey-type roses in the grass. The place was in good repair and a woman there pointed out a wood-road which led to the Pownalborough courthouse. Once this lonely house had stood in the center of the settlement, near church and parsonage, looking down across cleared fields to the river. Now it fought the encroaching woods—and ghosts—for existence.

As we drove home, Frances read from some of Parson Bailey's published letters which told of the hunger and nakedness of the people after the trade with England had stopped. There was no flour, no cereal for porridge, no greens, and no flesh. I can't imagine why they didn't have cornmeal at least, greens and "flesh," but Parson Bailey says no. People went to the clam banks and lived on alewives, "a diet on which they could not thrive." Where were the deer, and wild turkey—let alone tame pigeons and the farm cattle, sheep, and poultry? Had people no vegetable gardens? Were the colonies really so ill-equipped to survive? Parson Bailey goes on to say that clothes wore out and could not be replaced. Perhaps we have a picture here of a man isolated from his community, and unaccustomed to working with his hands, who depended on others for his food, and whose wife had never learned to spin and weave, and to whom no one else would either give or sell their produce.

Anyway, it is a very lonely picture, and it grew little happier when at last the family in their old, worn-out clothes boarded a sloop and sailed for Nova Scotia. Every turn of the river and every glimpse of an island filled Parson Bailey with the sadness of familiar things seen for the last time. In Nova Scotia he was met by a throng of well-wishers, for he was a well-known man and the Loyalists who had preceded him hastened to do him honor.

But he felt a stranger in a strange land. He longed for his house beside the church in a far-off place, and perhaps even for his stiff-necked congregation and the squire with whom (in the earlier days) he had so often argued so fiercely. But Parson Bailey never returned, and now only his pink roses and his white lilacs are left, and I must confess that I'm not altogether certain of even their genealogy. There are many pale pink roses and white lilacs in Maine.

But once I was strongly reminded of him, and perhaps for very little reason. Henry and I had walked through a field somewhat beyond the great house where Parson Bailey's contemporary, the squire, had lived, and so came to the broad Kennebec. There along the sandy shore below the bank and in the shallow water, grew a thousand cardinal flowers in a wide carpet of color. I had seen cardinal flowers before in streams, here one, there three or four, lighting up the flowing water with their brilliant torches, but never in this opulent, burning mass.

Suddenly I thought of the red coats of the eighteenth-century British infantry in the sunlight, and of the British banners flowing in the breeze.

Here was Parson Bailey's living memorial, a homage to his mistaken loyalties, to his courage and sufferings, growing almost never seen by passers-by, along the shore of the river he had so deeply loved.

Sitting Bull

ONE OF THE STRANGEST and most interesting visitors we ever had at the farm was a sewing woman, who for some summers toured the New England coast in a little car, stopping at each village for a week or two to make curtains and slip covers for people who found such work hard to get done. We have no sewing machine at the farm, so she did not stay with us, as I wish she might have done; we only saw her as she knelt by the old red plush chair taking measurements, or stood by the white iron bedsteads snipping out patterns in newspaper for the slip covers which were to hide the iron and transform it. She talked well and with charm, a charm which was part of her face and her carriage and the big floppy hat she wore and the loose gloves she pulled off as she entered the door. She was elderly; it was hard to say just how old, for every motion she made was light and swift, and she had that assurance which makes me think of the old French countess who said, when asked her formula for youth, "Oh, I have always been loved, and eaten fresh vegetables."

That charm, that seasoned gaiety, that knowledge that one is respected and safe from slights and indifferences—these are somehow rare things in America among the old. But she had them. She seemed to be without bitterness or fear, and her stories were delightful.

She showed us on the second visit (the visit with pins and fittings-on, that was) a photograph of herself in a habit and derby, riding sidesaddle on a good horse. She was still very fond of riding, she said; and that led us to talk of horses and of the old days. When she was a child, her father had been the Wells Fargo agent in New York. She was an only daughter, and he made a great pet of her.

"Fanny," he said one morning, "come down to the office around eleven. Sitting Bull will be there."

In those days the railroads once a year gave free tickets to New York to the chiefs through whose tribal lands the tracks passed, so that they might do their shopping in blankets, beads, red flannel, and kettles. Her father took charge of them while they were in New York. Little Fanny was not unaccustomed to seeing beaded vests in his office nor to hearing the soft slip of moccasins on his floors, but when she came in that morning dressed in her little bonnet and pelisse she met a glance of a dignity she had never met with before. Sitting Bull, with several lesser chiefs, was waiting for her father to be free to go with them to the shops which catered to the Indian trade. The old chief took her on his buckskinned knee and talked to her. He gave the child some keepsake (I do not now remember what), and later she stood on tiptoe at the office window watching her father walking down the street beside Sitting Bull, hearing the heavy wheels of the drays, and the stir of the coals in the stove behind her.

When she was sixteen her father took the family for a summer in Colorado. Fanny bought a horse for very little, because its tail was quite bare of any hairs and most buyers would not look twice at such a scarecrow. But it was a wonderful horse, fast, sure-footed, and easy-gaited. It had been a squaw's horse and was trained to kneel when it was to be mounted. Neither her father nor her brother could ride it, but it was perfectly gentle with her.

All summer she rubbed its tail with ointments; and by fall the hairs were grown in again, and there was no difficulty in selling her wonderful horse for twice what she had paid for it.

If she told us more, I don't remember it. Sitting Bull stalking down old Canal Street, the squaw horse kneeling to be mounted, remain in my mind with the exotic charm of the black-eyed Susans which grow wild now in our fields, but which Henry tells me are really prairie flowers which have worked their way eastward against the tide of immigration as the land has been cleared of forest between them and the sea. I never look at them without a faint sense of the buffalo herds, and of Indian tepees by a brown river; and so, when I think of the itinerant sewing woman, I see a shadow behind her of the West before it was quite tamed. But she herself chugged up our lane a third time quite casually, put on the slip covers she had made for beds and chairs, and, tilting her great hat and drawing on her driving gloves, drove away to return no more—neither to our farm nor to any of the villages which she had once visited like a migrating and solitary bird.

Haymakers

EARLY ONE MORNING, long before dawn, Henry and I were wakened by the wild torches of the lightning.

"Oh, the hay!" we groaned as we pulled ourselves out of bed to close the windows everywhere in the dark house. In July and August people's first thought is for the hay, the precious hay which has to be cut and raked and left to cure and carried into the barns. If a farmer hurries too fast, the green hay may smolder and set his barn on fire. If he waits until the hay is properly made, rains are likely to come up and ruin it. From one day of rain, hay may recover; two rains, and the stock may still be starved into taking it—cows vary greatly as to their fastidiousness; but a good spell of wet weather ruins the hay beyond any chance of using it, and it must be burned in the field, leaving long black scars parallel in the stubble.

"It takes courage to hay," I said to Mrs. Oliver, and she answered with grim gaiety, "Sure, it takes courage to do anything on a farm."

No one could watch our haymakers at work without being very anxious that the weather should befriend them. They come as a family, the farmer who works nights at the Bath Iron Works, and the thin quick-moving mother in her early twenties, wearing a light shirt and shorts. When her hair has not been given a recent permanent she looks like a back-road nymph, and it is she who drives the tractor. The eldest child is seven and a half, with a thin little face, pointed ears, and a wide smile. He takes his turn on the rake, raking the hay into long windrows. He did the same work last year at six and a half. He also treads hay on top of the truck while his father pitches. But he works only according to his strength. I happened to overhear a conversation last year which took place towards evening. Storm clouds were coming up, and the truck was half loaded when Odway started to slip off the hay onto the ground.

"Aren't you going to help me a little more?" his father asked. "It's going to rain soon."

The child looked up at his father.

"No," he said. "I'm tired."

That was all. No slightest pressure was brought to bear. Odway joined the other children.

For there are others: Ernest, now five, and Rowena, nearly three, and this year Cheryl, who sometimes lies on a baby blanket on our lawn and plays with the shadow of the apple tree, and sometimes sleeps in her carriage, in sight of her mother as she drives the noisy tractor up and down the slopes, hauling her husband on the reaper while the hay falls behind them in smooth blond folds like newly parted hair. Sometimes Ernest sits in the tractor with his mother, but usually he plays with Rowena.

I asked the mother how she chose Rowena's name, and she said with a little smile:

"I got it off a flour sack. Seems like there's enough people with common names. I like to give my children a name they can start off with."

If the boys have the pixy look, Rowena is a fairy. All afternoon she goes about with her pale hair making a nimbus of light about her little face. She has the fairy smile and blue eyes, and I have seen her go home supperless at nine at the end of a long summer dusk, as good and smiling as when she came.

The father keeps his eye on the children, and will walk across an entire field to tell them to keep farther away from the flowers. Once there were young bluebirds on the lawn, and he stopped work to bring a warning:

"Don't hurt those little birds, or I'll spank you. You mustn't hurt them, because they're pretty."

When he has finished for the day he takes all the children

swimming. Sometimes, on days when one of their uncles has joined in the work, setting their mother free, I have gone down by the lake and watched the three older children sporting in the shallow water by the alders. The Maine voice has a liltlike song to it, and they are like three birds splashing and calling from a shower of flying drops which catch the sparks of light against the green of the reflections.

So many things fight against the family. Their machinery is poor. Often the tractor balks or a piece drops out of the reaper or the rake, and you see them hunting for it in the new-cut hay; sometimes it is the gasoline which brings the work to a stop by giving out.

"Gosh, I was sure I had enough gas," Randall says. "Must have been lower than I thought." And next day they come back with a tin of gasoline, and the tractor coughs and starts again.

At first they didn't have a tractor, and Amos and Andy the steers dragged the reaper by day and stayed in our barn by night. Henry and I fed and watered them, and I liked to hear them low at the sound of our footsteps on the heavy floor. Out from the shadows of the tie-up their heads would come, their eyes rolling, their tongues twisting full length to wrap about the hay we brought with us. If we had water we had to push their greedy heads aside, and Henry got a bad scrape across a hand when it was caught between a flailing horn and the board face of the stalls. But any mischief they did was accidental. They are patient and kind, Holsteins, and Randall drives them with reins. It is a pretty sight to watch them working, walking as fast as horses, with the tall hay falling behind the reaper, and the robins and sparrows gleaning in the cut-over field.

As the days go on, with everyone watching the sky and wind anxiously, with the work threatened by thunderheads and put back by showers, with a march stolen against time by trucks loaded under the half-moon after dark, as the anxious beautiful days go on, our fields lose their carefree look and become neat and orderly. Still the children play about the house, and Frances, their mother, comes to sit in the kitchen rocker and gossip with Annie while she gives Cheryl her bottle.

This year after the late spring and a cold wet May the hay crop is thick and high. The redtop grass turns the slopes to a terra-cotta color. The weeds seem not to have flourished. And the haymakers are back, down to the baby. A good fortune upon your labors, one and all, and may the wind help you turning the hay, and the sun work with you, and the malicious rain be held back from undoing the labor of your hands! And may that troublesome tractor behave itself, and none of the children get sick! And let the rest of the machinery hold together and the loads not jolt themselves loose on the road!

The hay grows wild for the gathering, but the gathering is a long and uncertain process, especially when a man and his young wife are doing it with the aid of a child not eight years old. But in two years I have not heard one angry word or one fretful tone. You would think to listen to their voices that it was all some sort of long picnic on which they were embarked. We live during these weeks in the heart of a backwoods idyll, but all too soon the last hay has been roped to the truck and carried away, with Frances at the wheel and Odway holding the baby, and the other two waving, and Randall following, driving the tractor with the rake jolting after.

Morton's Woods

SOME PEOPLE SAY that it was a Forty-niner who had made his fortune and was on his way home to one of the back-country towns up the river. He had come as far as the Mills and must have arrived in the afternoon. Apparently he had struck it rich in California, for he sported a big gold chain and a fine watch which he looked at often. He let it be known that his family would be surprised at what he carried in the bag in his hand. Excitement had made him talkative. Excitement made him unwilling to stay at the Mills till morning, as a sensible man would have done. No, he must start for home, immediately, on foot. He didn't mind walking.

But night overtook him in sparsely settled country where the poor woods-farms are scattered at long intervals along the rutted road, and at one of these he must have stopped and asked for lodging for the night. Nothing more is known of him, except that he never reached home and there is a story of a schoolteacher who for years opened school and conducted classes with the aid of a great gold watch which lay on her desk and which none of the pupils ever dared to touch, although often enough they wondered what initials, if any, were cut into the case whose back they never saw.

But this is not the usual story they tell of the haunting of Morton's Woods, the long stretch of green which lies between Damariscotta Pond and the Sheepscot River on the unfrequented back road. In the days when people drove buggies, young couples were always warned to see to it that they were through the woods well before dusk, and surely with good reason if the tales of what people have beheld there are true.

This is a story of the Yankee peddler, that romantic and often tragic figure in our nineteenth century, about whom legends cling in every part of the East. He came from the unknown and passed into the unknown, bringing with him the gossip of the whole countryside, messages from up the road, and a cart filled with enticement for man, woman, and child. He was usually a being of great force of personality, of wit and persuasiveness, a teller of tall tales, a liar with his tongue in his cheek, and he must also have had courage, for he stopped at very out-of-the-way doors and had with him not only a cart filled with merchandise but a wallet filled with money as well.

All that is known of the peddler of Morton's Woods is that he stopped at old man Morton's and never went on again. But there was no proof of foul play, and no one to demand justice for a stranger. Still there was talk. The occasional neighbor, stopping to chat, found Morton's poor kitchen spruce with new tin pans, and a fresh broom always behind the door. The womenfolk had new calico dresses and the two big sullen Morton boys had new axes when they went chopping in the interminable woods that stretched beyond their walls. Some people went so far as to claim that they recognized the horse which did their plowing and hauling, and had last seen it between the shafts of a peddler's cart. But though the talk went on as country talk will, no one did anything about it, or probably ever would have.

However, as the months went on and the years, a change took place in old man Morton. He'd been breaking up fast, as everyone noticed, and he seemed uneasy all the time, as though his conscience wasn't sitting well inside him. He began to drop hints of dark things on his mind, and people noticed one or other of his boys always kept in earshot to give old man Morton a black look and shut him up when he began to talk that way. But the old man took less and less heed of them and their looks. His business appeared to be with his Maker.

Then one day the neighbors heard that old man Morton was dead. His family buried him without asking anyone in to see him. They said he'd died of a stroke.

The countryside thought that over for a while. "Stroke," they began to say when they'd thought enough. "Like as not it was a stroke of an ax in the back of the head. Those boys of his was real anxious about what old man Morton was going to say next." And again no one did anything about it, for it was after all strictly a family affair.

But if you were to take the old back road after dusk you might to this day see a terrible thing. Out of the bushes an old man with a flying white beard would burst, and go running stiff-legged across the road, his coattails flapping awkwardly behind him. And almost before you had had time to see the ax buried deep in his white head, another figure would jump out of the woods and take off after him, with *his* coattails flapping, and an ax in *his* head too. The second man would be younger altogether and go racing after the first in long revengeful bounds, so that you would say that he must come up with him any minute; but terror would somehow keep the old man just out of reach, and for as long as you dared listen you would hear the two crashings move farther and farther off through the dense woods, on the other side of the road.

Which explains why no one chooses that route after dark even with a car, unless he has plenty of gasoline, good tires, and headlights he can trust.

Oxen

THERE IS one daughter in the Simmons family and ten sons. They come of mixed Yankee and Waldoboro Dutch stock, and the young children of the family have skins of such rose-leaf pinkness and such milky whiteness that they might be little princes and princesses.

The boys have worked out as farm hands until they have saved enough money to marry and settle down on their own farms. We have been fortunate enough to have two of the younger sons with us, Lawrence, who won the Silver Star in North Africa, and for two years Ellis, later part of a gun crew at the Boston Airfield. They are brown-faced, strong-backed, pleasant-looking boys, but the handsomest of the family is Steve with his shock of yellow hair, his bright blue eyes, and his quick smile.

Steve is a raiser of oxen. He always has at least two yoke, and now he has a tiny pair of calves which he is breaking in for his little boy. Ever since we first came to the farm, Steve has plowed our garden, and I have memories of watching through flowering apple branches the deliberate motion of the oxen, the slow rolling-back of the earth from the plow, and Steve behind them with one foot in the furrow and the other trampling the sods down into place while Lawrence walked hieratically beside the beasts motioning with his goad. I have happened upon Steve against a skyline, working two yoke together at the plow, forcing the heavy earth. And at the fair the children and I have applauded him at the drag where he usually competes and wins in the middleweight class.

The oxen we knew best were Star and Lion, an unmatched team, rather thin, and with none of the Roman beauty that some of the greater oxen display. Star was black and white, Lion a brindled yellow. Year after year Steve threatened to sell them.

"They're getting old," he'd say. "I could sell them as working oxen, but they might get where they wouldn't be fed proper, and they've been too good workers for me to want that to happen. No, I'll have them butchered this fall."

But the next spring when we heard the heavy rumble of the cart which held plow and harrow coming along the lane, we would all run out, and the children would shout with relief and joy:

"It's Star and Lion again! It's Star and Lion!"

We knew them so well—which one ate salt and which one didn't, which one liked to go swimming and which one didn't, which one lay down to rest and which one remained standing. Kate learned to feed them and drive them, to know on which shoulder to tap an ox when she wanted him to turn, what to yell when they were to stand still or back up, even how the great blue yoke was put on and taken off. By the time she was ten she was a competent ox-driver. When the plowing was finished that June, we all got into bathing suits and Steve drove Star and Lion, yoked, into the pond. They waded slowly out, deeper and deeper into the water, obedient still. Now the water was up to their shoulders, now it covered their backs, now they were swimming, necks outstretched, eyes rolling a little. Steve swam beside them with the children swimming too. They made a great curve, startling the loons, and then waded ashore to browse on young leaves, up to their knees in water.

But next spring another pair, far prettier than Star and Lion, came with Steve. They were sturdy, well matched, and clearly colored in red and white. Their names were Broad and Bright, and they stayed at the farm a whole week, hauling logs and taking the blue cart down into the woods to clear brush. Henry and Pug, the dog, and I rode in the cart, seated on some hay, along the wood-roads, and nearly had the teeth jolted out of our heads. But we have rarely enjoyed ourselves more, and never have

I been so impressed as by the beautiful precision with which the slow, loosely harnessed animals manipulated that wagon down roads just wide enough to clear the axles. We had lunch on a rock over Deep Cove, while the oxen slowly ate their grass among the pines. They were so bright in their coloring that the shadowy pine woods didn't darken them. They looked like the charming toys old farmers whittle out on winter evenings. But they were not like Star and Lion to us. We didn't know their habits. They didn't go swimming with their master.

The following spring Steve was using still another pair. He had sold Broad and Bright to an old man who wanted them for hauling logs out of his wood lot that winter. Somehow one afternoon the old man slipped and fell between the animals and the slowly moving and heavily loaded sled. He yelled to them to whoa as he felt himself going; and without moving one step farther they both stopped.

"If those two steers hadn't been so well trained, I'd not be here today," he told Steve. "I'll never butcher them. They can live out their lives and die of old age."

There is a strong feeling here between the drivers and their oxen, although it is never forgotten that when a horse is old he is no good for anything, but that an old ox still makes good beef. The Maine farmers are realistic, yet many an ox dies in pasture. I remember once having tea under the big locust tree at the Halls' next door. Among the guests there was a young couple, who had traveled much abroad and knew the great cities of the world, but had roots in this countryside.

The talk happened to turn to oxen.

"I always remember a wonderful pair my father had," the wife said. "They would do anything he told them. He didn't have to shout at them ever. He had a cord, not much more than a string, attached to one of their horns, and he could lead them anywhere by that, without using the goad at all. He was very proud of them, of course. Then the last war came along and they were offering high prices for beef to send overseas. There was a mortgage on the farm which worried Father, and the price he could get for the oxen would just about pay off the mortgage. He talked it over with Mother and made up his mind to sell them.

"He took them down to where they were loading a livestock freight car. A lot of other men had brought their oxen too. They had to go up an incline of boards—like a gangplank, you know—into the car, and the men were having a terrible time getting their oxen up it. They seemed to know something was wrong. But Dad's oxen trusted him, so they followed him right up as though they were just going into the barn. And that always troubled him as long as he lived, the way his oxen had followed him that day."

Local Train

WHEN WE first came to the farm we used to wonder if the glimpse of the little local train stamping occasionally across its trestle beyond the sawmill pond at the end of the bay might mar the rural enchantment of the scene. But as we lived here we found that the old-fashioned hootings of the engine at the crossings, the sight of its puffing steam at night sometimes mingled with the glow of fire, the rattling passage of its two passenger cars and one freight, were a very integral part of our country day. Often as we sit on the sun porch at breakfast we listen to the westbound morning train climbing the grade through the woods, panting as it comes. A friend taught us what engines say.

As they climb they reiterate slowly:

"I *think* I can, I *think* I can, I *think* I can." And when they have reached the top of the hill they hurry down, exclaiming: "I *knew* I could, I *knew* I could, I *knew* I could."

This is certainly true. Since he told us, we have often heard our engine say exactly the same thing.

By day we like to watch its bustle and self-importance breaking into sight through the pines. For a minute it is in plain sight as it passes over the bank-beaver's house, and then it is lost to view beyond the fold of the hill. By night under the stars it takes on another aspect, and sometimes when the loon calls and a thin moon is shining I have seen it burst from the thickets like a maenad, shrieking and trailing its torch of fire and smoke against the sky.

By day or by night, we love it. May the time be long before any streamlined diesel engine replaces it!

Our conductor is a host to his passengers. He has traveled from Rockland to Portland for many years; he knows almost everyone who gets in and out of his cars, and has a word for each; and, if one be a stranger, he gives him the especial courtesy due to a stranger and stops to chat about the weather, the scenery, or the news of the day. The engineers share this relationship to their countryside. We have friends whose house is directly over a deep railroad cut on a river headland. They have no next-door neighbors but the trains. When our friends first went there to live they began waving to the engineers as they passed, and the engineers tooted their whistles in salute. The custom became fixed.

"At night, if we are in bed with the lights out, they never whistle. But if any of us happens to be reading late, they always give us a greeting as they go by."

All this is Maine of Maine. I know of no part of the world where people are kinder to one another, or to strangers. Our little train is a Maine train. It is not impersonal.

The other day Barbara told me a railroad story of the old days, of the 1870's, I imagine. A young woman was going visiting, dressed in her best, with bonnet, basque, and bustle. She was a rather timid soul, but after some consideration she decided to follow the line of the railroad track for part of the way, as it was very much of a short-cut.

I don't know just where this scene took place but in my own mind I see it as lying between our flag station and Butter-and-Eggs Bridge. Here the track runs under a long ridge out of sight of any of the farms, with woods and hayfields on one side, and deep woods on the other. There are very seldom section men at work, and, except for the switch, it is a one-way track. A passer-by might expect to see blue jays and possibly a woodchuck on the bank but not much else.

The young woman decided to save herself the two or three hills of the road and its windings by walking along the railroad tracks, but I imagine that she was uneasy. The loneliness made her uncomfortable. Suddenly she saw a couple of men ahead. What she had counted on as almost impossible had happened. In that solitary place she was going to have to pass by two unknown men with unknown intentions. She was torn between an impulse to hurry by, and another impulse to turn and go back the way she had come while there was still time.

Just then she heard the men shout unintelligibly and saw them beckon to her. The worst had happened! The poor girl turned and fled.

At that moment the engine charged around the curve behind her, the engineer rammed on the brakes, the section men gave a last helpless shout, and the cowcatcher caught the young woman and flung her through a four-board fence and into a field.

By now the train had squealed to a standstill and the engineer and fireman and shaken passengers and the two section men were hurrying to the lady, where she had been tossed in the grass. They expected to find her dead or dying, but she was miraculously alive although she had broken a rib or two in going through the fence. The cowcatcher had caught her on her bustle, that noble contraption of steel and whalebone, which had taken the blow and saved her life.

"Next year she married Father Oliver's cousin," went on Barbara, "and only died about fifteen years ago of a shock; and people said then, that it was the accident must have caused it."

I computed quickly.

"As the accident happened at least fifty years before she died, I should think that the shock might be due to other causes."

"Yes," agreed Barbara, who never argues. Still I am sure she thought to herself: "Being hit by a train *is* a shock. And she died of a shock, after all."

And so the lady did. People in Maine have long memories.

Pound for Pound

EVERYONE has been talking about the Waldoboro bear. Although many things have come out of the Waldoboro woods on their long ridges, no bear has been so much as caught sight of for a hundred years; and this creature came boldly into the middle of the town and was killed in the chicken yard of a man who lived three doors above the Baptist Church.

The man had been missing chickens for a week or more, and on a large scale. In a time when chickens were worth their weight in silver, he had lost nearly two hundred. One evening he and a friend heard the warning outcry from the hen yards and ran out, carrying a light shotgun, thinking that a skunk or weasel had got in among the flock. What reared up to confront them in the twilight was a big black bear. The man with the gun shot and wounded the creature in the head, then ran to a neighbor's, borrowed a heavier gun, and killed the bear in four shots. It weighed a hundred and eighty pounds—a formidable adversary to meet at one's back door in a peaceful village on a summer evening.

One late afternoon when Irving Oliver brought his big white horse, Major, to cultivate the acre of potatoes he had planted on a slope of our hayfield, he stopped after work for a few minutes' talk. We asked him about the bear.

"I saw it myself," he said. "Went to Waldoboro shopping, and everyone I met asked, 'Have you seen the bear?' So I went up to Sam's place. He had it hung up in his barn, and, gosh, it reached from the ceiling to the floor. All black without a white hair on it, and thighs as big as a man's. They sold its meat at Gay's at forty-five cents a pound. I didn't want it. I don't hanker for bear's meat, or raccoon's either, though some like it."

"Has there ever been a bear around here?" we asked.

"Never in my time, nor Father's either. But I guess now there's another somewhere around. Where you find one, there's likely to be its mate."

When our neighbor had gone, we speculated upon how much salable meat there would be on a hundred-and-eighty-pound bear, and concluded that perhaps there might have been a hundred pounds. But we were counting without the meat famine. The next time I found myself across the counter from the butcher at Gay's store, I asked him how many pounds of bear meat he had sold. He laughed.

"A hundred and eighty-three pounds from a hundred-and-eighty-pound bear. We sold it bone and all, just as it came. Yep, a hundred and eighty-three pounds it came to, from a hundred-and-eighty-pound bear."

I doubt if the pioneers ever did better than that.

Molly Molasses

PERHAPS NOTHING is ever quite lost. But in Maine old things linger on more visibly than in many parts of the land. So it does not seem particularly curious that every year the Indians come to us selling baskets. Many things at the farm are kept in Indian baskets which must have been peddled at the same door fifty years ago. Nowadays they drive in cars, and the style of the baskets has changed subtly to meet the modern taste; but the fundamentals are all the same—the wide ash splints of the heavier baskets and, for the smaller ones, the edgings of sweet grass which only the Indians seem to know where to find.

The Maine Indians were always a rather peaceful people, often preyed upon by the Mohawks from what is now New York, who came on raiding expeditions from time to time. We have become acquainted with several families of Old Town Indians. I am interested to notice that it is the wives who remember the Indian words for things which their husbands have forgotten. They are hard-working, quiet women with a smiling look. They say little, but their husbands seem always to turn to them before making a decision. I remember a room in an Old Town house with sixty or seventy Red Paint axheads and fishing weights spread on the floor. It was a question as to whether we could buy a single piece. The man sat back on his heels, his fingers unconsciously tapping a drum tune on the floor boards. He was considering. No, he would not part with the curious ball of iron, shaped like a head. But perhaps a duplicate stone shell? Before he decided he glanced at his wife in the doorway. She did not speak, nor nod, nor smile; but a sense of "Yes" flowed from her like light, and he sold the shell-shaped fishline weight.

I remember another scene, not in Maine but in an Indian village on the lower St. Lawrence. The man had long thin mustaches and a watch chain strung across his open vest. He was a Montagnais, but his wife, the tall woman at the stove with a man's hat on her head (that was once the old fashion with squaws all over the East) came from that very northernmost tribe of Indians, the fierce Nascapi, who in the past so often warred upon the Eskimos.

A member of our party wanted to buy for a museum the drum which the man had. I think he was willing. The hunting had been bad the year before, and he must soon be getting more supplies from the Hudson's Bay Company for the winter's trapping. The Montagnais, men and women and children, spend their summers in villages on the river; but in September they return to the northern forests and, breaking up into small family groups, hunt and trap all winter, living in tents.

So when the chance for a trade came the man hesitated. He spoke to his wife, this time in words, and she answered, speaking at some length, with an expressionless face. Her husband translated what she had said into Montagnais for the priest who was with us.

"They hunt alone," the father explained, turning towards us again. "She says that when night comes he plays upon the drum, and it is like the beating of her heart. She does not want him to sell it."

My closest acquaintance, however, is with an Indian woman long since in her grave beside her husband, Neptune. I was writing a book on the early Maine of 1817, just before the state broke off from Massachusetts to begin a separate existence. I was reading town histories and other simple local narratives, and among them was a little book published in 1860 or 1870 which mentioned an Indian woman named Molly Molasses who had once saved a white man from drowning, and who was considered as something of a prophetess, because she had foretold a great future for a newborn baby who in due course of time became governor of the state.

The name caught my fancy. Molly Molasses! Into my book she should go. It never occurred to me that within her own sphere she was an historical character with her own connections and associations, but later I was to receive a letter which startled me. It was from an elderly woman now living in the South. I have mislaid the letter, which told the story far better than I shall tell it. The writer was a white woman and had been born in Bangor where Molly Molasses was then living. Molly was a friend of the family's, and when the baby was born the Indian woman asked if she might be godmother. Her presents to her godchild were more than silver cups and leather Bibles. She gave the newborn girl a beautiful woven belt, and the power to curse and bless. The child knew only about the belt as she grew up. She was twelve years old before she learned what else had been given her.

At that time her family had a young dog, which one day leaped up on a neighboring child and scratched him with its claws. The child's father demanded that the dog be shot, although all the children of both families begged for its life. But the man was overbearing—he was a member of the police force and something of a bully, as well—and the dog's owner shot it rather than have trouble over the affair. Not content with issuing his order, the neighbor came into the house at suppertime to make sure that he had been obeyed. But there he went too far, had he but known it. Seeing the little girl red-eyed at the table, he began to make fun of her for crying over a dog. She jumped to her feet.

"As there is a God in heaven," she cried, "may I live to see *you* ruined and in tears!"

When the man had gone her mother scolded her.

"You must be careful what you say," she told the child. "You have the power to bless and curse, you know."

The girl had not known. She listened eagerly to her mother's account of her godmother's gift. When in a few months she saw the neighbor ruined and in tears, she believed in her own power. And all her life she has felt it within her—the Indian woman's gift, the power to curse or to bless.

I am continually fascinated by what interesting people live all about us. The world is a wider and more exciting place for holding in it a woman to whom Molly Molasses bequeathed her gift. Since reading the letter I have seen a portrait of Molly's daughter in a Bangor club, an Indian belle with beadwork ornaments and bright-colored flounces. And a year or two ago an Indian woman showed us Molly Molasses's cross—a French Cross of Lorraine in silver, as I remember it. The woman, who was her great-granddaughter, said that Molly Molasses had worn that cross to the day of her death; and it was touching to hold it in the palm of one's hand. But what was a silver cross inherited by a great-granddaughter to the gift she had given to her white godchild, the gift of power, the black magic and the white?

The Pukwudgies

LEANING IN THE CORNER of our parlor, at one end of the haircloth sofa, is a tall staff made of some very light wood, with a notched pattern around the handle. I am very fond of using it when climbing what we call our mountain, where now white pines grow over the old pasture land and only the deer use the paths through the woods which once the cattle shared with them.

Our Neck cattle have always been wanderers, finding their way to Deep Cove for their noonday drink, standing during the noonday heat in glades among the pines, following single file along their narrow paths, their tracks mingling with the tracks of deer and upon occasion of moose. To them a fox is nearly as well-known a figure as a dog; their bells have startled the partridge; the rabbits have bounded away from their slow approach. Here the wild is always present, circling the tamed, protecting and at the same time menacing it like some unpredictable forest deity. Perhaps that is one reason why Henry and I are conscious of Indians as the race created by this land, why he enjoys talking with them, visiting in their villages, wearing things which they have made, while very few books of mine have appeared without an Indian in them, as a kind of seal or signature.

This staff against the flowered parlor wallpaper is fifty years old and was made by a half-breed Penobscot named John Snow who used to live in one of the coastal villages, weaving baskets for the neighborhood women.

John's father was white, his mother was Indian. In his mind the old stories and traditions lay in dimmed and broken images; yet, as a sort of gypsy dweller beside the white men's houses, he still remembered something of the tales which his mother had told him as a little boy. He remembered about the great sea monster, and about the small people known as Pukwudgies. They stood no higher than a man's waist, and their heads were long, or so said the few who had seen them, for they were shy, and hard to get a glimpse of. They would visit a hunter's camp while he was away, and if they were in a good humor they might cook him a dinner and leave it for him to find simmering in his pot over the coals of a fire; or they might scrape a hide for him, or do some other kindness. But if something had happened to put them in a bad humor, they would upset all his things, throw his supplies into the bushes, hide the blankets—there was no end to their mischievous tricks.

The Pukwudgies were childish, but they were very wise. They knew the future, and if one approached them properly they would answer questions. As a man John Snow remembered that his mother had once taken him as a little boy to a rock near the mouth of the Machias River. There were old marks on it. She might have brought a present with her—he could not remember; but he did remember that he and she stood by the rock, and that she called out a question and that the Pukwudgies answered it. Was it Echo which spoke? If so, surely an Indian Echo.

Shells and Red Paint

THE GREATEST Indian shell heaps in the United States are heaped on either side of a small rapids in Damariscotta River. They make two high white moraines which shine brightly between the green of the water and the green of birches growing above. People stop on the highway to look down across the fields at them. A few make inquiries and follow the small path over a fence and down to the water's edge. Seen close at hand, the shells seem more gray than white; and it is surprising that many of them are oyster shells, no longer found in the river at all. With a little digging, especially perhaps where a woodchuck has loosened the mound by his labors, one is sure to find whole shells. Naturally one looks too for possible arrowheads or bits of broken pottery; but, though the mounds have been excavated at various times, not much has been found in them.

Not only have scientists dug here, but the road-builders have used this wonder freely for surfacing new roads, making far smaller an irreplaceable landmark of the past in the wasteful American way. The other day the old Damariscotta photographer showed us a picture he had taken twenty years ago of an Indian skeleton found by the road-builders. It was seated, facing the east, and there were about it a few stone weapons, shards, and wampum. The wonder to us was not that so few skeletons were found, but that there were any at all, for one does not expect to find Grandfather buried under the kitchen table.

There seems to be no doubt as to how these shell heaps were formed. The Indians of Maine led a life in pattern much like that still followed by the tribes along the lower St. Lawrence. In winter, after the harvest of what corn they had been able to grow and the autumn killing and curing of meat, they broke into family groups to follow the game into the forest during the starving months. An entire village could not survive, living together; but the small units, wandering here and there, largely succeeded in getting through the harsh season, and returned little by little to their villages on the rivers when spring came.

After planting their cornfields they moved down to the seashore or to the head tide of the rivers to enjoy the fishing and the clams, mussels, oysters, and lobsters which they could gather so easily then. There were established places for eating the shellfish, and great heaps of shells are found up and down the coast where the tribe year after year sat and ate their fill, throwing away the shells as people do today. They also dried clams and oysters to take inland with them; but the Indians' prudence could never be on a very large scale, as they were limited to what they could carry on their backs. Fortunately, they were not given to worry. They lived while alive, ate while there was food to eat; and these shell heaps are the memorials of their days of plenty when food was easy to get, the work for the women light, war far away, and the children played like little brown frogs in and out of the shallows.

These shell heaps were still being added to in historical times; people like to calculate how many hundreds of years they must have taken in the making. The lodges of the Eastern Indians are gone; their arts, largely vanished; their trails are a fading memory. Only the stone axhead and arrowhead turned up by the plow in the farmer's field, and these simple domes of shells are capable of resisting the elements for a long time.

Here in Maine there are earlier, stranger memorials, too, of a lost race, which we call the Red Paint people. From the days of the first settlements, men now and then have come upon a mass of iron pyrite powder, buried in the earth. Occasionally a pioneer mixed some of this into paint and colored his ladderback chairs, his stair rail, or his door. Often they did not know that this red powder marked a burial so old that even the bones had turned into dust; but now and then fragments of bones were found, or spearheads, or fire flints, or stone sinkers for long-ago fishnets. I have seen a hundred such objects laid out on an Indian floor in Old Town when a burial place of this earlier people had been happened upon in road-building.

For the Red Paint people are not supposed to be the ancestors of our Indians. There are no arrowheads among their implements. They knew only the knife and spear. But they knew how to strike sparks from stone, which our Indians did not know. Some people believe that their villages, nearer the water than their burial places, were drowned out in the sinking of the coast; some think that they made their way northward and are now the Eskimos.

The other day we were driving past the house of an acquaintance who is a chief of the Old Town Indians. We stopped to talk, and he showed us a fine powder horn decorated with the pattern of the double curve, the early Algonquin design used before the French sisters taught the Indian girls a version of the Jacobean flowers and hearts. It was a beautiful horn, worn with use to a mellow gold. Henry thinks it is older than the 1849 scratched in a space in the pattern. Perhaps the same hunter who dated it, added the small cross more deeply etched than the rest of the design and extraneous, as though put in as an afterthought, perhaps for extra luck, or perhaps to add a Christian check to the old magic of the down-curving animal horns.

After we had seen and admired this our friend brought out half a dozen skin scrapers, spearheads, and such; and it astonished me to find that Henry knew from what regions had come the stone of which they were made.

"That's from Mount Kineo," he said, and our friend nodded.

But the most interesting thing in the collection was a long narrow javelin head, nearly seven inches long and less than an inch across, beautifully shaped from a smooth gray-green stone, like shale, but harder and not split. On one side the stone had been grooved with a pattern of slanting lines, narrowing to nothing as the point narrowed.

"I found them," said Joe, "after there had been very high water in the river. The river had washed away the bank. I was walking along, and I saw the point of that long stone sticking out of the bank. I walked on, and then I thought, 'That must have been something.' So I walked back. I dug them all out together. What good are they to me? Those scratches may represent people, the number of people in a village, perhaps enemies. That was our way of keeping count."

To us it looked like simple decoration; but Joe is more likely to be right. Was it not Powhatan, the father of Pocahontas, who sent one of his chiefs to England with his daughter to count the White Faces there and to bring him back word of their numbers? The poor barbarian kept tally in this way with notches, until, as he walked the streets of London, he saw that he would never have done, and so threw his tally sticks away in despair. We shall not know what little village somewhere numbered thirty-eight warriors, nor to whom or why the information was important, if that *is* the meaning of the pattern. Henry thinks that the work is Red Paint. If so, the mystery is deepened, and the hunter who carried it was of an unknown race.

The Innovator

FROM THE BEGINNING witches have always been connected with the stock. When the cow sickened, when the healthy calf died, when the ewes were barren, people looked about for a witch to blame. Annie tells me of a cousin of hers whose cow was drying up. She cut off a hank of hair from its tail, tied it in a bundle with needles and pins and witch grass, and boiled them all together on the stove.

Her father watched her sardonically.

"I should think you were old enough, Sally," he remarked, "to know what's wrong with your cow, without trying to drive out witches! Her calf came at the beginning of March, and no wonder you don't get much milk."

Mrs. Rollins once told us a very vague black tale of a wizard who lived and died here generations ago.

"He was a man witch," she said. "Oh, I don't know how long back 'twas, but 'twas a long time ago. My father always said they hung him because he was smarter than they were."

"What did he do?" we asked, the shadow of an old stupidity, an old wrong, already overhanging our thoughts.

"It don't sound very sensible," said Mrs. Rollins briskly, "but I'll tell you the way I always heard it told. It seems in those days when people went to the mill they went on horseback with the grain in a bag on one side of the crupper. Then to balance it, they put a stone in a bag on the other side. The poor horse carried double weight. Well, this man thought of putting half the grain, or of the flour as the case might be, in one bag and t'other half in the other. It was much more sensible of course, but it was a new idea to the people in these parts. That's all I ever heard tell that he did; but they hung him. Maybe there was other things, but they're forgotten. Anyway, my father always said that they were a pack of fools, and he was the only sensible man among them."

Can it be that this tale has come down from the earlier settlements? A belief in witches there has certainly been here, and that within the lifetime of the old people; but surely hanging goes back to times earlier than our village. However, to either side of us lie very ancient settlements. Samoset, who met the Pilgrims, deeded land at New Harbor to an Englishman, and Sheepscot is one of the earliest outposts of white men in the New England wilderness. Who knows where the witch man lived, and thought up the poor contrivances for which he paid so dearly?

Young Katahdin

THE PROFESSOR is what a professor should be, learned and merry. Perhaps he has remained so human because his interest is in human beings, preferably Indians, and preferably Eastern or forest Indians. We sat at the table on the sun porch overlooking the lake, and he lighted a cigar after breakfast and talked.

"Don't you wish to live with Indians who have no white blood, and no white ways?" Meg asked, deeply interested.

"No," said the professor. "I like to find odds and ends in a man's talk by which I can follow back to the old beliefs. I am satisfied when someone tells me how his grandfather twice met the great water serpent on Eagle Lake and he and his companions had to lie down in the bottom of the canoe so that they might not die from breathing its foul breath. I can reconstruct the past when another man tells me how his great-uncle when hunting came upon tracks in the sand by the river which were like a man's in shape but were as long as a gun. Then he knew that the giant was out with his pack-basket on his back, looking for young people to carry away to eat, and he went back and broke up his camp and traveled as far away from those footprints as he could get."

The professor likes young people. He saw Meg's eyes dark with interest, and went on:

"Shall I tell you the story they tell at Old Town about the girl who was lonely? At the western end of Indian Island there is high land from which you can see the mountain of Katahdin seventy-five miles away, especially on a clear evening. This girl was lonely, and she did what the young Indian boys and girls do when they are lonely. She went to the top of the rock and sang a lonely song every evening, something like this:

Young Katahdin, I hear you are very handsome.
Young Katahdin I wish that I might meet you.

"One evening when she had finished her song there was a stir in the bushes, and a handsome young man joined her, saying, 'May you live for a long time.' She had never seen him before, and after a while she dared ask him who he was and whence he came.

"He answered her frankly:

" 'I am young Katahdin, and I have heard you singing to me every evening. This evening I thought I would come and take you back with me to be my wife.'

"She was very willing, but wished to go down to the village for the consent of her father and mother.

" 'No,' the young man said. 'I am not like other men. If you wish to come with me, you must obey me. Put your two hands on my belt and close your eyes until I tell you to open them.'

"The girl wished to go with him, so she took hold of his belt and closed her eyes. She felt herself rise up and up into the air. Then the wind roared past her, and in a short time her feet were again on the earth and young Katahdin told her to open her eyes. She found herself standing near the top of the mountain by a great cliff. Young Katahdin stretched out one hand and drew back the rock like a deerskin, and they went into the mountain. Inside, a fire was burning; and his family was there, his father and mother and sister.

" 'This is my bride,' said young Katahdin, and his family made her welcome among them.

"She lived there for four or five years very happily, especially after the coming of her little boy, Katahdin's son. He was like other boys except that he had cheekbones of stone to mark him as the child of the mountain. He was very strong and active.

"One day the Indian girl said to young Katahdin:

" 'I long to see my own people and to show them our child. I never said good-by to my father and mother, and the thought troubles me.'

" 'I will take you back as I brought you,' said young Katahdin. 'But remember: you must never say an angry word while you are there.'

"So the Indian girl took the child on her back in a basket and closed her eyes and put her hands on her husband's belt, and when he told her to open her eyes she was standing on the little height of island where she had once sung the lonely song. When she went down into the village she was welcomed as one who has returned from the dead, and the child was greatly admired.

"Day after day, week after week went by and she lived happily with her people. But one day young Katahdin's son was playing with the other little boys of the tribe, when he shot a blunt arrow which bruised another child's cheek. The hurt child ran bellowing to his mother, who, in the manner of mothers, ran out and shook Katahdin's son, scolding all the time.

"The Indian girl who had married young Katahdin, hearing the uproar, also ran out. 'What is all this?'

"The other woman began to scream her reproaches; anger roused anger and in a moment young Katahdin's wife had said a bad-tempered word.

"No sooner was it out of her mouth than young Katahdin stood beside her and took her and their son away with him once more. They were never again seen in the village; but sometimes a solitary hunter on the outskirts of the mountain will meet another hunter whose cheekbones seem made of granite. Then he greets the stranger with extreme politeness, but slips away as soon as possible, for he knows that the man is not human, but the son of young Katahdin, and that his temper is a little uncertain."

"Did young Katahdin kill his wife for speaking angrily?" Meg asked.

"Oh, no," said the Professor. "He just took her back to the mountain. He felt she'd been visiting long enough."

Fair Wind

THERE WAS a woman who lived in Damariscotta about the middle of the last century when it was a center of shipping and exported to most of the world the oak and pine of its woods, the ice of its lakes, and the red brick made in the yards along its riverbanks. She kept a sailors' boardinghouse, ostensibly, but on the side she had a good trade in selling winds.

Although one thinks of a witch, particularly a seaport witch, as a rather cosmopolitan person, this woman seems to have retained a good deal of local pride. So one evening when she heard two captains in her boardinghouse boasting of their respective vessels, which were waiting ready-laden for Boston, and of their general handiness and remarkable speed, she naturally took the side of the Damariscotta captain—the other was an outsider from Bath maybe, or maybe Bangor. Anyway the woman made some excuse to call the Damariscotta captain out of the room, where he sat arguing with the other man.

When she had him in the darkness of the hall, she whispered to him fiercely:

"Bet him all you have, and I'll give and I'll give and I'll give you a wind, and you'll be in Boston by morning."

That sounded pretty impossible even to the Damariscotta captain, but when a witch told you to do something in those days you did it, and asked no questions. So he went back and laid the bet with the other man and then roused up his crew and went down to his vessel and hauled up anchor in the dark —or what dark there was, for the moon was rising. There was a downriver wind rising too, of which there'd been no hint earlier in the evening, so they made good time with an outgoing tide. When they sailed into the ocean a strange thing happened:

the following wind veered into the east—it was still a following wind. There was no tacking, no shifting of the course to keep the sheets filled, nothing at all for the captain and crew to do but set all sail and dance down the coast while the cook put the coffee to boil on the galley stove. Hour after hour went by, and the wind never faltered nor shifted again. Like a big broom sweeping a ball of paper before it, that breeze carried the Damariscotta vessel straight to the entrance of Boston Harbor and then, with a sidewise flick, it tossed her in.

The moon was gone and the morning star was just beginning to pale and there was light on the eastern horizon when the ship came in to its usual berth at T Wharf after such a voyage as no Maine vessel ever has had before or since.

"Got in kind of early, didn't you, Captain?" asked the watchman, holding his lantern for the captain to step ashore.

The captain nodded.

"Had a fair wind," he said laconically.

The Cabinet

IT WAS a summer Sunday morning, and we were driving up the river from the bridge, past the great square-pillared mansion that looks down the green tide-rip of the river to the twin towns at the head of navigation. It is a wonderful example of the Greek Revival house of the 1840's, with a very beautiful fence. We knew it was empty and had been for some time. It was undoubtedly at my suggestion that Henry stopped the car and we walked up the weed-grown path, and stood under the square pillars looking down the river. After exclaiming over the beauty of the scene, which although part of the villages is also part of the great natural sweep of the tides and the life of the river, we turned humanly enough to look into the double parlors through the long French windows beside us. But we saw more than we had bargained on, for there looking out at us, as close to the inside of the window as we were to the outside, was the long distinguished face and the long lean body, dressed in a white linen suit with a flower in the buttonhole, of the owner of the place. He, too, had dropped in for a Sunday visit, but with a good deal more right than we. However, he flung open a door and invited us in.

The parlors were twin rooms, with marble fireplaces and Brussels carpets. Curtainless and high-ceilinged, they were rather austere, as the rooms in many Greek Revival houses are. It was easy to read the tastes of many masters there. A stuffed bobcat and raccoon stood on the bookcases; a caribou head leaned, wistful and curious, from the wall above the piano, and a rack made from the horns of various types of deer and gazelle waited for coats and hats in the wide hallway. We had heard that the man who was showing us about could walk through any woods at night without sound and without hitting into the trunk of a tree or the branches of a bush, that he knew the ways of all birds and creatures.

"We used to be allowed three deer, two caribou, and one moose by the old game laws," he told us. "But the caribou are all gone now, shot off. The last herd was driven over a cliff on Katahdin. A pity they don't restock it sometime."

I can't remember where the elephant's-leg footstool had come from, with the hay bursting from the seams.

But perhaps you have an idea of the rooms—old-fashioned, long unused, smelling of dampness, and clearly belonging to men who had loved horses and hunting. In the second parlor, however, one came up short, before something very different. Between the long windows was a high cabinet with glass doors, apparently French or Italian. Inside and out, it was of buhl, dark tortoise-shell inlaid with gold and silver. There were designs of eagles, crowns, seraphs' heads, and intertwined monograms.

"I don't know anything about it," said its owner. "Don't care for that kind of thing myself, you know. Wouldn't read a book if you paid me. Rather look at something real any day. But I do know that after the Siege of Paris one of my grandfather's captains brought this back. Been in a palace or museum or something. Can't remember who it was made for. Oh, wait a minute. It's written down somewhere."

He fished behind a red-lacquer Chinese vase on one of the shelves, found nothing, felt behind its mate, drew out a paper.

"H'm! Just as I thought, one of those French kings. Here, you can see for yourself."

There it was, made by—an Italian name which I forget—"for Mme. de Montespan by order of Louis XIV."

So that was that. We traced the monograms in gold and silver under the crowns. But our host was not much interested.

"Don't care for that sort of thing myself," he repeated. "However, I was good and mad one day when I came in and found it moved halfway across the room. Neighbors told me a truck with two or three men had driven by here one evening. Neighbors didn't think anything about it at the time, but the men in the truck must have been after the cabinet. I waited for them with a shotgun for two or three nights, but they didn't come back. I guess they found it heavy. Don't care for it, as I said, but don't like to have my things stolen, either."

The buhl cabinet was back in its place in an empty house, above a vesselless river. We sighed, as we went out again to the sunlight and the high-pillared veranda.

Mostly Ginger

ANNIE lives a life of marvel. The cat which her daughter took back to the city from the Rollins farm next door has not had a life like other cats. I saw him as a kitten, a big fluffy deep golden ball with all four of his paws double. I have never seen him grown up with his heavy coat and sweeping tail, but I know what a fierce hunter he is, and how he will leap and catch a ball five feet in the air. I know too what a baby he is, accustomed to a great deal of attention, and how he will come when his mistress blows a whistle, leaping over back fences and streaking across back yards, startling anyone whom he may pass. But the other day when Annie spoke about the time Ginger brought back the diamond, I was surprised.

"We were in the kitchen," Annie explained, "when Ginger came in limping. He'd apparently got something stuck in the soft hair around the pads of one of his hind feet, and he sat down on the linoleum and stuck his foot out and began pulling at it with his teeth in that way cats do. Pretty soon something dropped out and Olie went over to see what had been bothering him.

" 'Why, look at that,' she said. 'It looks like a diamond.' So when Johnny came back from work she said to him, 'Look at the piece of glass Ginger brought home in his foot.'

" 'Glass!' said Johnny who once worked for a jeweler. 'That's not glass, that's a diamond.' "

To make sure, he had it tested. It was a diamond all right. Olie put an advertisement in the Lost and Found column of the local paper, but no one ever answered it; so some day she's going to have it cut in two and add a small diamond to each side of the one in her engagement ring.

"That's a cat worth having," said I.

If Ginger is a cat worth having, he's not the only cat who has brought money to his mistress. Half the farmhouses of our neighborhood have Maine shags playing about the sheds and barn doors, and the women make a little money from the sale of kittens, which are collected and sent down to pet shops in Boston and other cities. The prevailing rate of pay at the farmhouse steps is two dollars for a girl kitten and three for a boy, although a fine white kitten with blue eyes may bring as high as five dollars. No one knows where these "shags" or "coon-cats" originally came from, although Wiscasset claims that the captain who tried to rescue Marie Antoinette, and who sailed home instead with a hold filled with palace furniture, was the very man who, on another voyage, brought back a pair of Persian cats, from which all the long-haired cats of Maine are sprung. Maybe so. At any rate they are thoroughly at home here, and live hardy, little-cared-for lives, although often they retain the look of palace cats as they walk the stone walls in search of chipmunks, or sit in a sunny corner of a tumble-down barn.

There is an old story from Westport Island of a cat—whether long- or short-haired—which kept a family alive during starvation times with the man away fighting the British, by bringing back icefish from an open place in the ice of the Sheepscot River where a spring flowed up. Many a cat has brought back rats—why not "icefish," whatever an "icefish" may be? Certainly one fall during the war we became acquainted with a very gentle gold shag. The weather had turned cold with heavy morning frost on the fields, and when the loons swam in our cove they left behind them two widening lines of skim ice. We were saving gasoline as was everybody else, so we went out little and had few visitors. One day as I walked down our lane to see what deer had crossed it in the early morning, I noticed a thin yellow cat with a very fine feathery tail hunting in the field. I didn't call to it, thinking it must belong to one of the neighboring farms, although it was wandering rather far from home; but that afternoon it came to our shed.

Close at hand, we could see that it was almost starved to death. For a week we fed it continually. Like most Maine cats it would eat anything, cereal, bread and milk, table scraps—anything; but for a long time this poor cat could not be filled. It was very gentle and well mannered, never showing the slightest greediness, starved as it was. It was altogether at ease with Pug, although Pug regarded it with some mistrust. We named it Yellow Brother, I think.

At that time the chief heat of the farm came from a big ornate stove in the dining room which Henry called Lillian Russell and which kept warm all night on coal. Pug had his wicker dog-basket beside the stove, but when Yellow Brother would step into it Pug would step out instantly, looking thoroughly disgruntled. I remember on that first evening I found in the shed a carton, rather small and high-sided, into which I wedged a small sofa cushion. For anyone as flexible as a cat, it would do very well temporarily. I remember the scene when we took out the lamp, with Pug on his cushion in his basket on one side of Lillian Russell, and Yellow Brother blandly slant-eyed in his box on the other.

But how different was the scene when Henry called me to see it next morning! Now it was the cat which stretched at its ease in the basket as though upon display, and the black, wrinkled and disgusted face of Pug which appeared in the box where he lay wedged tight between its four sides. He had to be pulled out, as a cork is pulled out of a bottle, and we could never guess how Pug—who is nothing of a climber—had ever got into the carton without knocking it over.

We began asking about our guest and letting it be known at the grocery that a stray cat had come to us, and one evening an old Ford hammered up to the door in the darkness, and a woman in the slacks and wearing the button of a worker at the Bath Ironworks appeared in the doorway and asked almost fiercely:

"Have you got my cat?"

I stood my ground.

"What color is it?"

"Yellow."

Then I led her to the kitchen, and in a moment more she had Yellow Brother in her arms.

"I thought he had been poisoned. They were poisoning rats around an empty house just below us," she said. She wanted to pay me for our care of him.

"What's his name?" I asked.

Her face took on a slight look of embarrassment.

"Baby," she said.

Together we worked out Baby's adventure. That fall he had been bringing up in the shed a litter of little half-brothers and -sisters, a year younger than he was. And then one day they had all been sold to the cat dealer. Baby had disappeared that evening. He had gone to look for them. He had looked for them for three weeks, through the woods and fields, apparently almost without food. And when he could look no farther he had come to us.

Among the rather devil-may-care cats of Maine, Baby had the gentlest spirit I have ever met with.

Maine Quality

YESTERDAY we were visited by a friend whose great-grandfather and great-grandmother built a farmhouse looking straight down the Medomak River to the sea, over the dark backs of a dozen islands, and there raised their thirteen children. Every one of these, boy or girl, went to college. The mother found time to weave blankets from the wool of their sheep, and napkins with colored borders from her own flax, and the processing of flax is long and tedious.

Some years ago I was told of the stone doorstep of an old house which, upon being moved, showed hidden under it a bundle of flax nearly rotted away. The owner believed that it had been buried there during the French and Indian Wars to preserve it for a return which never took place. Damariscotta and Nobleboro were among the settlements completely abandoned during those terrible years, and it would be strange if this hidden flax were all that has come down to us besides the records to give a picture of the despair and frugality of the colonists preparing to flee in their sloops and ketches to shelter on the outer islands—that is, those who were not killed in their fields, or carried off to a Canadian captivity.

I know very little about the actual raids in this neighborhood, except the story of a little boy who lay hidden in a Waldoboro cellar hole and so escaped the massacre of the family; and there is a long rock, dark with seaweed, in Damariscotta River on which two women were killed, running I suppose down the long slopes and out into the water, hoping for help from some passing boat from the upper settlement.

Of Pemaquid Point and its fort and the siege and massacres there, I know more. There was, for instance, the little girl who was scalped beyond the fort and lay all day on a pile of stones in the hot sun, and lived to tell the tale, for between the summer sun and the heated rocks the bleeding of her wound was stanched; and she was alive when they came to bury the dead, and wore her cap into old age with grandchildren at her knee. There was young Giles too, who was carried into captivity. His father, who was killed at the time, was an influential man and the son of a wealthy merchant of London. I always remember what Giles's mother said to the boy, speaking out of a long silence as the canoe in which he was being carried passed the one in which she sat. They were being paddled straight eastward to round the point, eastward towards the open sea which lay between them and England.

"I would that I were going now to my brother's great house in London," she said, "and that he were but there at the door to welcome me home."

I know of no words ever spoken which give one such an insight into what the women of the colonies felt. These painted savages, these uncouth shores of rock and spruce, the unpredictable future—how came she to be in this nightmare, whose place was at the window of a London house, embroidering in the afternoon light while a servant spread the cloth for dinner?

Ah, this ocean, this ocean! How it joined the continents, and how it separated them too! Here at Pemaquid early in the seventeenth century the *Angel Gabriel* was wrecked, and many were drowned, although the majority of her crew and passengers were saved. Among the survivors was a man who was preceding his wife as a settler to the new world; but the shipwreck so terrified him, and his descriptions of it so terrified her, that she could never find the necessary courage to join him. Nor could he ever return again over the sea which had so frightened him; and they lived out their somewhat timorous lives on opposite sides of the Atlantic.

But I have wandered far from what I had in mind. Our friend, the granddaughter of the youngest of the thirteen children, has a neighbor who is quite deaf and a little inclined to be gruff. The other day a man came to the neighbor's door on a rainy day to make some inquiries. The stranger stood in the drip while he shouted his questions and received his answers. Then suddenly the farmer invited him in:

"Thought you might like to have a little drink of something in the kitchen."

As the city man stood gratefully steaming by the stove, sipping his whiskey, the other eyed him benignly:

"We have a saying in these parts, 'If you wet a board only on one side, it'll warp.' "

Isolation

ONE OF THE OUTSTANDING features of pioneer life was and is its frequent isolation. I know of two cases myself where a family has been marooned without its men, and faced starvation waiting for their return. One case was on lonely Matinicus Rock where there is an old lighthouse, and the old stone keeper's-house, now abandoned, still stands looking out over the sea towards distant Monhegan and the Main.

The keeper and his family and assistants live a little farther down the slope towards the boathouse and the runway. There is no shelter at the Rock. If there is any sea running one cannot land a boat there. The place is only a few acres of tumbled slabs of stone between which grow wild angelica and other island weeds, shading the nests of a great colony of terns. The air is filled with these birds and their cries and their sharp-cut neat bodies slicing down towards one's head, while their pink beaks (which match their pink feet) snap to and fro like scissors. They are a violent cloud of wings overhead to the stranger, but the lighthouse people grow very tired of them and their nests, and wish that a way might be found to keep them from fouling the cistern water on an island where there is no spring.

I have been on Matinicus Rock and climbed carefully over its difficult terrain to see a small colony of puffins, here called sea parrots, which have chosen the most remote outpost of cliff to perch on. I have seen the fringes of its rockweed rising and falling with the waves, and heard the loud spouting of a passing whale. They told us how, about the time of the Civil War, a keeper had rowed ashore for provisions and was caught and held on the Main for twenty-seven days of gale, during which his young daughter took his place, tending the light all night through, and showing great courage and foresight in running out during the full terror of the first storm to rescue the chickens which were to stand between the family and starvation in the long days to follow.

That is a story of which Mrs. Cruickshank has written in her charming *Bird Islands Down East,* illustrated with photographs taken by her husband; but I heard it told before I read it in print. The other story of isolation is more anonymous, and the dreary little drama was played out in an old house on Westport Island which friends of ours have taken. If Matinicus Rock is almost like a wave shattered and frozen into granite far out to sea, Westport Island is a mere fringe of land in the Sheepscot River which has become detached from its shore. It lies far up from the sea in the tidal waters, with its farms and woodlands and coves. One still has to go to it by a ferry, pushed along a heavy cable by a capable powerboat. There is still at the foot of the hill the old board giving the tariff for neat cattle, for ox teams, carriages, and sheep. The ferryman goes to his lunch at half-past eleven and returns at half-past twelve, and woe betide the man who wishes to cross the river while the ferryman eats. His motor horn will sound in vain, for long years have inured the ferryman to calm in the face of impatience.

Once on Westport Island, the road wanders for some miles to the small village at the far end. But the lane to our friends' house branches off through the woods, a mere vein of a road, dipping down over a stream which they have now dammed, and so coming out to cleared fields and two houses commanding a fine broad view down the river. There is a cove and a reef where the seals bark, and near the water the gray shingles of a ship's chandlery. Life came by the river in those days, and the big house is clapboarded on the two sides which might be seen from the water; but the humbler shingles would do to face the lane. The place has wonderful cellars too, and fireplaces large and small. The sons of the present family catch lobsters, often cooked by the edge of the water where the stream enters the river and two great mill wheels lie on the rock. The original mill was a shingle mill: once cedar shingles were made here for the West Indies trade. Farther down the river there is another gray chandler's shop, which, according to tradition, was for some time kept by a woman living alone, who sat at the counter with a gun laid across her lap.

Now the story which they tell of this tall river-fronting house is for me dated only by the Revolution. The companion house had not been built at that time. The clearing stood alone, and its family lived alone; and when the man went to the war they were left quite alone there, locked in and barred by the forest.

Time passed, and the man did not return when he was expected. Had something happened to delay him, or had he been killed? There was no way to know. It was winter now, and the food in the kitchen was very low. There was no chance for a woman and little children to get more from the woods, and the deep snow barred them from their distant neighbors.

Every day they ate less and less, and then came a cold bright morning when the woman put the last of the cornmeal before the fire and made the last johnnycake. There was nothing more to eat. The family stood about the table to say grace, and it must have been a desperate and poignant grace which was said. As one of the little girls raised her head, she saw through the window her father plodding across the snow dragging a heavily laden sled of provisions. And when all else about them has been forgotten, the tradition of that grace remains, as much a part of the house as the bricks of its chimneys and the wide boards of its floors.

Abraham and Betsey

IN THE EARLY YEARS of the nineteenth century there lived in Damariscotta a couple named Abraham and Betsey Tilton. They must have been filled with the high spirits and overflowing courage of a new nation; they loved a laugh, and they probably relished both excitement and danger. During the War of 1812 the British fleet lay off the coast of Maine and foraged the farms for food, and sometimes fought villages which resisted, and once or twice even burned them—although anything so unsportsmanlike as burning a dozen houses and a church, though without the loss of a single life, was frowned upon by the liberals in England.

Muster Day then was of great importance; booths were set up along the street, and the whole countryside drove in to see the drilling. Gingerbread and rum were sold in great quantities; there was much skylarking; the country girls who had walked in from the farms carrying their shoes so as to keep them out of the dust put them on and stood by the town pump and giggled at their acquaintances marching by. The local gentry appeared on horseback; Squire and Captain were usually synonymous. There were peep-shows for the children and perhaps a monkey on a string, or play-acting in a booth. Muster Day was one of the great occasions of the year, when, all through New England, the people counted their strength against time of danger, and displayed their skill in drilling and firing their muskets.

One Muster Day, Abraham Tilton appeared carrying a broom instead of a musket, a tin funnel instead of a powder horn, and a bunch of turkey feathers in his hat instead of the regulation porcupine quills used for cleaning the barrels after firing. Every time the officer gave an order he shouted out a sailor's "Aye, aye, sir," and soon had the bystanders and militia in such gales of laughter that he had to be dismissed and ordered home before the muster could proceed.

The same high spirits which made him play the clown helped him upon occasion to play the hero. It was sometime during the War of 1812 that he and Betsey were running ammunition to Boston in his schooner. The hold was filled with boxes addressed to Andrew & Barstow, the famous ship chandlers. Each box was marked with a large *A & B*. As the little vessel slipped between two islands, it was stopped by a shot across its bows from a British frigate. Subsequently an officer came on board with drawn sword to find the most tranquil scene: There on the deck, with the cat at her feet, was Betsey knitting, her wide skirts modestly spread about her, totally concealing the powder keg on which she sat. She went on knitting, she went on sitting, as the officer stepped below with her husband for a glass or two of Madeira in the cabin before giving a routine search to this family vessel. I suppose the idea that a young man would take his wife with him on a dangerous voyage scarcely occurred to the Englishman. Betsey knitting on the deck above was guarantee enough of the innocence of the cargo. He did not know his Americans.

The talk in the cabin was pleasant; the Madeira, excellent. In a golden mood the officer took his stooping way into the hold. On every side were boxes marked *A & B*—"for Abraham and Betsey," explained the master of the vessel blandly. They were moving to another dwelling, and these boxes held their household goods. The polite Englishman nodded. Certainly.

He had seen the ship's papers—*Abraham and Betsey*. Quite reasonable. He returned to the deck, bowed over Betsey's hand, climbed down to the waiting gig.

Betsey sat where she was, smiling and knitting, knitting and smiling, as the sails caught the wind once more and their vessel gathered headway.

The Carver's House

EDBURY HATCH was late in finishing his training as a carver of figureheads and ships' scrolls and decorations. The great days of the sailing ships were almost over. When he received his papers as a master craftsman he had barely time to carve two or three ladies in tight bodices and high-buttonned shoes, with flowing tresses and wide wind-swept skirts, before the demand for such things was over forever, and he was left to decorate a few doorways, and lavish his art upon the small white house where he lived with his two unmarried sisters.

In this house he had been born. His father, a sparmaker in the shipyards below, had paid for it over a long period of time, and had raised his family in it. The house itself does not look over the river; but the boy, Edbury, going for the cow or gathering raspberries for his mother at the back of the yard, would have seen the entire port below him at one glance, and all day long the air must have been filled with the sound of axes, shouts, and the tapping of hammers sheathing the sides of some vessel on the ways.

I have no idea where or how the money came into the family; but when we met the old sisters, after his death, they were well off. We went to call on them and were invited in and shown over the house. Inside and outside, it was adorned by Edbury Hatch's care and affection. He was a rather crusty, unneighborly man, people say. When his sisters wanted a telephone they had to wait until he was away for the day before they had one spirited into the house—to meet him as an accomplished fact upon his furious return. He was shy and avoided people. But love he certainly felt, if only love for his craft and his dwelling. In its heyday three carved porches adorned its three doors; a large carving of the seal of the State of Maine hung on a blank wall of the ell; there was a waterspout like a dragon's head; a carving of sunflowers decorated a small skylight in the roof, and the eaves of the barn were fringed with a waving drapery of wood, extremely graceful.

Inside, we stepped into a Yankee house of flowered carpets, gilt mirrors, and coal stoves—but, oh, how different from other houses! for nearly all the furniture had been made by its master, the mirrors had carved frames, and so had the pictures. Some of the work was beautiful; I remember corner brackets held up by bouquets of mingled flowers which were charming. But sometimes his taste weakened. Kittens played up the frames of several pictures brought back from Japan by a brother who was a ship's engineer, and sailboats raced in low gold relief across the top drawer of a bureau. The eagles on some of the mirrors looked more like winged carrots than birds. Oh, it was easy to smile, but the entire effect was delightful. Where else in the world was there the house of a Yankee figurehead carver?

When the old sisters died, the brother who had been an engineer inherited the place. He sold his big place higher up the hill and came to live in the house where he had been born. He was rich by village standards. One day the old man asked the advice of a friend of ours.

"What would you do in my place, Fred?" he said. "I've got a good deal of money in the bank and not many years to live. I'd like to make the most of the time I have left."

The younger man had his advice ready.

"Why don't you buy a car and hire a chauffeur and go down to Florida?" he asked. "No use trying to save now."

The old man listened thoughtfully and nodded.

"Yes," he said at last. "That's what I say. Why save now? And I act on it, too, Fred. Nowadays, when I walk down to the village, if I feel like an ice-cream soda I don't think about it twice. I just walk right in and order an ice-cream soda, Fred. Just like that."

In a few years he died. We tried to save the house as it was, but neither town nor any society could undertake the expense. A niece in the city sold all the furnishings to a dealer; the man who bought the house as an investment took off the porches. The figurehead house is scattered to the four winds of heaven. Now, as one drives past, it would be hard to guess how unique it was a few years ago. Only the sunflowers still bloom above the glass skylight, and the wooden drapery flutters from the eaves of the barn; both are too high to be easily reached, and so, like a last apple left at the end of a bough, they remain at least for a little while longer.

November

THE OTHER MORNING, going to the kitchen door neither early nor late, I saw a fox trotting across the upper field past our graveyard. He heard the sound of the opening door, glanced over his shoulder, and trotted on, neither faster nor slower. I was pleased enough to see him, but a good deal more pleased two or three mornings later when I saw him again, this time hunting for his breakfast. My coming upon the scene did not disturb him in the least, nor did the arrival of Henry and Pug. For an hour we watched the charming spectacle. He was evidently catching grasshoppers and mice, more often grasshoppers. He would walk quietly towards a bunch of grasses, then pounce, prettily and neatly. Once he sat down for quite a while, his ears cocked forward listening. Most of his coat and brush was red-gold, but his hind legs and the upper part of the brush were a good deal grayer. Such a distinguished visitor, with his air, Henry said, of a British colonel without the monocle.

Almost every day now in November we see something interesting. The other evening there were whole regiments and companies of crows flying very high against a cloud-flecked sky. The late light was burning on the pond and along the eastern shore, and the water reflected russet and green; and there, far above, the crows winged silently, endlessly coming out of the east, endlessly flying into the sunset.

It was only the next evening that a porcupine came up very late from the cornfield and walked close to the back door. We couldn't resist going to meet him with our flashlights, and he lumbered off at a rather pathetic trot, slowing down out of breath at the rise of the field, until we were sorry for him and stopped accompanying him, so that he might at leisure waddle home to inform other porcupines of the glorious skill and daring with which he had outwitted us.

In this year of no apples, the pears on the old tree on the terrace have been of unusual interest to me. They have spotted skins and are too hard to eat—or perhaps we don't keep them long enough—but they make very nice stewed fruit or preserves. Henry scorns them until they appear for dessert or with the breakfast toast, but I have a particular affection for them as a kind of fruit Cinderella. This morning I thought, "Now I'll pick six more pears," for I had left twelve on the tree. But when I walked out in the clear cold sweet air I found a chipmunk in the old tree and another waiting in the grass below. The thief in the tree was so intent on his work that he held his ground as I came close, and we looked at each other, eye to eye. Then, in a sudden panic, he scampered off.

But where were my twelve pears? Only two were left, too few for human use.

"Keep them," said I. And, as I turned, the chipmunk hurried up the tree again while his companion waited below. I almost saw her spread her apron to catch the pears when they fell.

But, as many have said, every life is a tragedy ending in death. I have to teach myself to accept this, especially with our deer. All summer the doe and her twin fawns have been robbing the gardens, leaving their clear-cut hoof prints in the damp earth. I have found their track in the woods and by the lake; they have crossed our road almost daily, and of late we have seen them more and more often. They had been unmolested and were accustomed to stand waiting for a car or truck to pass. A few days ago at dusk they stood under the great maple with the lightning-blasted top while a car went by, but this time there was a gun beside the driver and the doe was shot. I stare as I pass the flattened ferns and hardhack where she fell. Louise, hearing the shots, looked out of her kitchen window and saw the fawns walking slowly side by side across the Hathe and at last into the woods. They were being fired at, but that they did not understand. What they did understand was that their mother had not followed them.

All this seems to me a sad end for that precise and visionary beauty whose presence has added a grace to all our days. When the rain fell I used to wonder in what deep thicket the doe and her young were sheltering; in the early morning I wondered where they browsed. But I can see that a farmer cannot support a herd of deer in his fields, even if he enjoys a sight of them now and then. And I know, too, how much the venison means in a country household. Nothing is wasted; the hanging shelves in the cellar bear an added burden of jars filled with venison mincemeat long after the last steak has been enjoyed. The fawns, Henry says, are old enough to fend for themselves, and in this snow they must now be carrying on their precarious lives as best they can.

Well, then, deer must be killed, ours as well as the deer ten or a hundred miles away; but I am more reconciled when, as in this case, the shooting is done by local hunters for the enrichment of Maine larders. On two November Sundays this year we have happened to be on the main highway going east, against the traffic of Massachusetts cars returning home with their spoils. There is still a kind of tragic beauty to the figures lashed to the front mudguards; the gutted does with the ropes knotted above the hooves and across their brown backs; the stags with their antlers like branches of the forest. Sometimes a fawn will be tied across the bumper in front of the radiator. A few fasten extra carcasses on top of the car or pull them behind in a trailer. I have seen five deer festooning a single automobile—so much life and grace and beauty come to nothing—while inside five men, or men and women, sit humped over in their Mackinaws and red caps, stupid and inert, or so they seem to me.

Surely there should be a proportion in killing as well as in other things. This procession of death, driving westward towards Boston, smacks of the slaughterhouse and stains the clear beauty of these November afternoons. Almost twenty-five thousand deer have been killed in Maine this season, and most of them by out-of-state hunters. As to the number wounded, but not killed outright, one hates to think. I wish that, before a hunting license was issued, the hunter might be required to show his skill, as a motorist must pass elementary tests before getting a driving license. To allow people to get their training on the animals and game birds themselves seems to me barbarous.

A Matter of Principle

IN A COVE of Casco Bay, we used to visit a friend who lived in a very out-of-the-way log cabin just above the sea. The road dropped down to it through woods whose floor was soft with moss. There was an inner pool of salt water reflecting cloud shadows and tree shadows—but, oh, how cold that clear water seemed, and how the barnacles scraped our skins as we sidled down the rocks into it! The genius of this particular place was an old fisherman who kept his dory and nets near by, although the house in which he lived with his daughter and son-in-law stood above on the road. It was to old Andrew that our friend turned in any difficulty; it was he who told her where to buy firewood, or who among the neighbors would be best to mend a leaky roof. He grew to be very old, but still he came down to his dory and went off to his fishing. I always liked his rule that you must fish from the right side of a dory, because Jesus had so commanded the disciples.

"If you fish on t'other side, you get some queer bad things in your net," he told us quite seriously.

The daughter with whom he lived had been married first to a fisherman who was always spoken of as "having been lost at sea," although he could be seen about the streets of Portland any day in the week. In due course of time she married another man, a fine lobsterman and fisherman; but Andrew never approved of the marriage and refused to speak to his daughter's new man.

When his own wife died, Andrew was left with no woman to take care of him. He turned to his daughter as the next of kin. The fact that he refused to speak to her husband seemed not to alter his rights in any of their eyes. Surely in another part of the country the old man would have had to agree to let the causeless feud go before he came under his son-in-law's roof; but not in New England. Perhaps the younger people hoped that Dad's ill-humor would wear off. If they did, they underestimated the obstinate nature of the old man. For thirty years he lived with them, and never to the day of his death addressed a word to his son-in-law. For thirty years his daughter cooked for him, mended his clothes, and set his place at the kitchen table between hers and her husband's. For thirty years the big lobsterman stamped in, pulled off his sea boots, answered his wife's questions, lighted his pipe, and with patience endured the old man's silence.

Dad's right to be crabbed if he was by nature crabbed was respected in that simple household. And after a long life of hard work, of sea fogs, and islands rising from a crisscross brilliance of water, of chapped hands, and of nets and lines always thrown to starboard, old Andrew died, with the satisfaction of knowing that he had never weakened nor addressed one word to that fellow Abby married.

Sheepkill

WE LOOKED CAREFULLY at the stoves, got into our warm coats, caps, and mittens, and went out. Our snowshoes stood patiently on their tails in the snowbank by the door and with them strapped to our feet, the banked hill slope was easily descended. The lake looked like a marble eye, white and expressionless. We crunched across it, the rackets of our snowshoes leaving two precise patterns of tracks in the snow behind us. They were like leaves crisscrossed in Jacobean embroidery, growing on an invisible vine, except when I blurred the pattern by stopping to tighten a strap.

It was a March day, but the thaw had not come yet. I think it must have been early March. There were no white lids of snow on the dark pine trees, no tracks on the level snow of the lake. From where we walked we could see no house or be seen by none. We seemed to be in a clearing of the forest, entirely alone, with no other sound than the squeak of leather and the crunching of the snow.

At the opposite bank we climbed steeply to the railroad track and negotiated with care a barbed-wire fence. We were now in the Vannahs' pasture with its huge solitary oaks. Climbing still, we came to the hayfields, and so to the house and its two large barns. I don't remember where we met Hudson. Probably Laddie, the collie, barked, and Hudson came out of the big yellow cow barn. I know that he took us in there, and that the cows looked sleek and lazy in the tie-up, and that then he led us down a wide ramp to the cellar under the barn.

It was lined with stone, had narrow windows under the ceiling and was filled with crowding sheep. Laddie went among them barking, and they moved about, keeping their staring eyes turned towards him. From the flock there arose the bleating of newborn lambs. Two or three had already been dropped—weak, small things uttering weak, small cries and covered with skins infinitely large and wrinkled. They were not pretty, they were not gay; but they touched me more than any skipping lamb I have ever seen in a green field. They were the first younglings of spring, born here under the ground, while the snow lay deep above them. At the moment they seemed like the epitome of all the roots and bulbs which strove in the darkness for the sun: they were hope in the womb of earth.

Later Hudson took us to the house to see his mother, who gave us hot gingerbread and glasses of milk, and we talked for a little; but the early dusk was already beginning, and we soon made our excuses and started for home by the way we had come. When we reached the lake, where now the snow lay blue in the dimming light, we found that another pattern had been added to the double vine left by our snowshoes. Now the pad tracks of an animal went along close beside them. Beginning at our bank of the lake some large four-footed creature had followed our trail all the way across. So must the track of a scouting wolf have looked. Of course there are no wolves; but we had never seen a dog on the lake, nor could we imagine what dog this one might be, so large and so persistent in its interest in us.

This small puzzle was one never to be solved. The woods are mysterious. They enfold the Maine farms, and all sorts of things come out of them: innocent things like the young porcupine which has recently been eating high-top apples every afternoon while we have tea at the table below; charming things like the deer which came with a herd of cows into the barn of a farmer near Jefferson, and which stayed with them winter and summer for nearly three years. And then there are other things neither innocent nor charming. The summer before we went over to see the lambs, we had heard the Vannah sheep bleating steadily from their pasture. Our telephone was working then, and we rang up Hudson to ask him if anything were wrong, for we knew that the wind would carry the sound our way and not his.

"I'll go right down and see," he said.

A few days later we heard the story. He found the flock huddled in a wall corner, and one sheep dead. It had been recently killed. He did not examine it closely, but drove the flock up to the field near his house where he could keep an eye on them, and it was not until the next day that he had time to return to the carcass. In the meantime the killer had been back. The sheep had been eaten, bones and all. Only the skull and skin were left.

"No dog could have cracked big bones like that," Hudson said thoughtfully. "Nothing I know of could, unless it was a bear, or a Canada lynx."

Again came that thoughtful pause.

"Aren't any of those around here either," he admitted. "But in September they travel sometimes. You can't tell what may come out of the woods."

"Is it likely to come back for more sheep?" we asked.

"Well, it might, unless it's going some place," Hudson said.

But the killer was never heard of again in our parts. It had struck once, and then vanished. No one ever knew what it was.

Background of Sea

AFTER a heavy southeast wind it has always been the fashion of this countryside to go to Pemaquid Point to see the surf. The rain has stopped, and the sky is blue overhead. The ocean is blue, too, but it comes against the striated rock in soaring walls which move forward neither fast nor slow, breaking in columns of spray, hard as stone and delicate as frost. There is a strong smell of seaweed in the air, and a continual low throbbing and booming.

"See the people," says Henry. "They look like the figures in a picture of a shipwreck," and they do, standing grouped about the lighthouse or scattered down the sloping cliffs. But they keep well up those slopes, for men have been caught here by a breaking wave and carried to their deaths when the surf was high. As for wrecks, there have been wrecks too, and even now we watch with some anxiety the two or three fishing schooners under reefed sail which plunge and labor by on their course. The far-off islands are ringed in foam, and the reefs are marked with white. The eye grows weary with the greatness of the scene and comes to rest on a sea gull in dark immature plumage riding lightly on the neck of a thirty-foot breaker. Yet these waves do not break like waves on a beach. They spring forward and upward along the cliff with the whole force of the ocean behind them. The motion is all leap, the leap of a lion, and yet unhurried, with a thousand elegant and lovely details.

Sometimes we all come here to watch the spouting of a pod of whales. It becomes the news in Damariscotta: "There are whales off Pemaquid," the storekeepers remark, and then we drive down to see the sight. And sometimes we merely come because the weather is fine. Then the lobster boats chug along close to the foot of the cliffs and men fish with long poles for rock bass, and sandpipers run in and out of the rock pools, flying on their short skittering flights, uttering their piping cries. I remember seeing an Indian here one day fishing with a white boy. It was the Indian who caught all the fish, and each time he drew in his line he would laugh out loud.

The other day we found men at work in the hayfield belonging to the lighthouse. There were so many boulders there, and the crop seemed so poor, that one would have thought the hay scarcely worth cutting; but on the headlands the people must take what they can find for their cattle. Two men, one of them quite old, were swinging their scythes among the rocks, while a boy was using a mowing machine pulled by a pair of half-bred Jersey steers, their cowlike heads fitted out with horses' blinders and bits, and their bovine flanks circled with breeching straps. The workers made a family group of grandfather, father, and fourteen-year-old boy, while the mother watched from the edge of the field. She told us that it was the boy who had trained the little steers, which were named Thunder and Lightning. Never did I see a gentler-looking pair, quaint and pretty in their big harnesses.

The background of sea, the sea gulls slanting by overhead, the oxen at work, the boy's voice shouting, the beat of the waves below on the cliffs and the sound of the bell buoy on the long reef which juts out beyond the end of the point, all combined to create that sense of man and his surroundings in harmony, in beauty, which alone can be the base of a real community or civilization.

Scaregull

FOR THE PAST two summers the gulls have come in to the lakes. Not only do we now have the sea fog standing up along our southeastern horizon, but we have the sea birds in such numbers as were never seen here before. When we first came to the farm a sea gull was a rarity. The Rollinses told us that they came in after blueberries. In ten years we never saw more than two gulls together, but last summer we sometimes started up fifty or sixty at once from the rocks beyond the islands at Deep Cove as we paddled by. How well we knew that white flapping of wings whose sound is so much like that of a flag in a strong wind! How well we knew that forward leap into the air and then the beautiful swerve of the whole wild flock and the cold high cry as they flew off! Sometimes we see a dozen in the cove below our fields, so many whitenesses against the blue; sometimes after sunset their dark silent shapes pass in formation over our roof, just discernible against the last light of day and the first stars.

We like these messengers from the sea, but our neighbors who come for a few weeks each summer to Loon Island like them less well.

"They eat the yellow perch," they say. "We used to be able to get a mess for dinner in twenty minutes, and now we have to fish for two or three hours, all thanks to the gulls. There was an article in the Portland paper saying that the depth bombs have disturbed their usual food and that they've come inland in great numbers to the lakes and rivers."

We are not fishermen, so we can watch the gulls without that dreadful rivalry of which the world is likely to know more and more. The only fish in these parts with which I have had a personal acquaintance—and that merely by hearsay—was the tame trout which Lawrence, our hired man, once put in his home spring to keep the water clear, a very old country habit. This fish was a mere fingerling when he was brought to the spring, but much feeding made him large and sleek. He was quite unafraid of people, and for him a human shadow across the water was a signal to rise for some gift of food. Lawrence and his brothers had quite an affection for their adopted trout, and they were all angry when one fine day they found the spring uninhabited.

"I suppose some fellow came along for a drink and saw our trout and went and got a hook and line and caught him. That fish would come up for anything. Sure, the man must have known he was a tame trout; but some fellows wouldn't care for that, as long as they weren't caught at it. I'd like to lay my hands on him, though!"

To return to the gulls, whose suave shapes and edged cries are now part of our daily lives, I remember their beauty once in a field over the sea to the north of us here. A man was plowing and the gulls followed him, sometimes flying and wheeling, sometimes settling in the furrow and walking after him like a flock of white hens. The horses bent their heads and pulled strongly. The old immemorial shape of the plow dragged at the curling earth. The man followed, intent upon his labor, his steps uneven in the soft new ridges of the ground, and overhead and underfoot streamed the sea birds, looking for insects and apparently welcome enough.

But recently I saw a scaregull, where the gulls were not welcome. It was off the point at Chamberlain, near that entrancing little island of stiff white rock and black spruce called Pinch-of-Tea Island. The fishermen have their herring seines there and do not care for the presence of gulls above the imprisoned fish. So, as a farmer sets a scarecrow at the edge of his cornfield, some fisherman has anchored an old dory near the seines with a dummy in it seated as though fishing. The figure wears a torn slicker and shapeless sou'wester, and with every week leans more and more towards the gunwale; but still, we are told, it impresses the gulls.

They have not had a crow's cynical experience with such things.

Captain Dekker

RICHMOND is a little forgotten town on the Kennebec with two streets of fine houses parallel to the river and a long history of ship-building, ship-sailing, and of the ice trade behind it, and apparently very little ahead. Across from it lies Swan Island with its woods and farms where legend says lived the lady sachem Jacataqua who followed Aaron Burr to the siege of Quebec under the leadership of that other controversial figure, Benedict Arnold.

I have never looked up the subject enough to know how much of the tale is legend, and how much "little" history, as the French say. What lies behind the account of the bear and her cubs killed by Burr with the aid of the young Indian girl? of the feast later and the toasts drunk there? of her journey through the wilderness mountains with the expedition, as official hunter? or of Burr's friendship with a British officer met with by chance at a spring in the forest, in whose charge he put his Indian mistress until her baby should be born? I have no idea if the beloved Theodosia Burr, the idol of her father's heart, who perished so mysteriously somewhere off the coast of the Carolinas —I have no idea if she really *had* a half-sister, with long black hair and bright black eyes, whose mother's people were settled on Swan Island.

The most interesting thing we noticed there was a very large wooden arrow fastened as a weathervane to the top of a pine tree growing tall and shaggy on the bank. The arrow of course marked the wind on the river, and sometimes bodies of water seem to have their own winds, differing from the land winds beside them. The arrow was so large, so old, and so noticeable that we remembered it when we later came to talk with an old man at the grocery store.

He was a relic of one of the great Maine trades, a retired blacksmith who had followed the camp-meetings in summer and the ice-cutters in winter. He remembered when a thousand buggies used to drive to the camp-meeting oaks back of the Winchenbaughs' at our own Nobleboro, and he told us that the farmers left baskets of high-top apples by the side of the road for the use of the camp-meeters, while the worldly swapped stories and horses, and the religious listened to the preachers on the outdoor platforms under the trees. His more important work was in shoeing the horses that hauled ice on the Kennebec. Two things have handicapped the Maine farmer, he said: the introduction of artificial ice, and the replacement of the horsecar by the trolley. Until then, a hard-working man could count on a thousand dollars a season for pressed hay—that's why our barns are so large. If he needed more money he cut some ice and shipped it somewhere in sawdust. This old man had lived in the era when the local farmer not only made his own living but handled money. After we had talked for a while, we asked him about the weathervane.

"Oh, that!" he said. "That was put up by Jim Dekker. His father was a captain, drowned before Jim come along. From the time Jim was a little boy he wanted to be a captain, too; but his mother wouldn't ever let him go to sea. He certainly loved boats and anything to do with water. He had two stores here when he died, and was pretty comfortably fixed. But that wasn't what he'd really have liked if he'd had his own way.

"Funny thing about his will. He had a nice powerboat when he died. He left it fixed so that his heirs could salvage the engine and any of the gear they wanted. He didn't care about that. But the boat itself they was to take out into the channel and saw right in two. Yes, it was all in his will; right in two pieces, he wanted her, and sunk. He didn't intend anyone else should ever use his boat. She was the nearest he ever come to having a vessel of his own."

The Promise

PEMAQUID HARBOR was the scene of much fighting during the French and Indian Wars, and the fort changed hands several times. A pirate named Dixie Bull once sailed up the river and attacked the town. Now it is a quiet place, with the rebuilt fort, an old garrison house, and an older graveyard to mark its past, and a few modern houses and a couple of piers where one may order boiled lobsters and eat them at long tables with the sandwiches and coffee which the wise bring for themselves.

It is less than an hour's drive from the farm, and we go there several times a summer, enjoying the different mood of the coast. The sea water sparkles and shines, like a thousand thousand minnows showing their silver sides to the sun. The islands look artificial on their platforms of rock, with their spruce woods clipped neatly by the wind. A lighthouse has the air of a freshly painted toy, and one can hear the mournful tolling of a bell buoy on a reef rocked by the swells. The gulls are an endless study in beauty and greed. They soar down from the sky or sit like ducks on the water about the piers waiting for the lobster shells to be thrown into the sea. Hoarse complaints, wild squabbles ensue; often enough a gull swims off, well weighted down at the bow with its share, its sharp, neat stern pointing upward. Or the gulls wade along the rocks collecting starfish. Suddenly a strong white head and Roman beak disappear under water, there is a sharp tug, and up comes the head again with a star in its tip, which is eaten with frequent immersions to help wash it down.

On sunny days the sea air has a gaiety about it, a wild invigoration commanding one to do something, to go somewhere, to seek the adventure just around the corner. No wonder so many men along the coast took to deep-sea voyages, and came to know all the great harbors of the world. In the little shops of Maine we have bought old trinkets from China, India, and Africa brought home by the local men. A man once told me that when he was a boy the small town he grew up in on the opposite side of Pemaquid Point was filled with monkeys and parrots from the Gold Coast. I myself have seen ivory tusks and carved wooden combs brought back in that trade; we know that one bold skipper hoped to bring Marie Antoinette, the Queen of France, back to Wiscasset. There was no end to the importations!

Opposite in the town of Pemaquid Harbor, on a slope of land looking straight down the river to the islands and the sea, there stands a large square house, well back from the road, behind an ornamental fence. There is a summerhouse to one side in a thicket of flowering bushes; a golden centaur weathervane tops it, his arrow pointing towards the sky. The big house is empty now. Its lawns are uncut, its garden forgotten; but even today it is the very epitome of a Maine sea captain's house.

Jake Day told us its story. The captain was a relative of his—I should only be guessing if I put a name to that cousinship or great-unclehood, but he was "in the family." Like so many of the men who went to sea as boys, he was a captain in his twenties, and by forty was prepared to marry and settle down to a life ashore. His young wife had a terror of the sea, and the captain gave her a solemn promise that he would make no more voyages after they were married.

So the wedding took place and the bride came to live in the big square house over Pemaquid Harbor, and a baby was either born or was to come. And then, like a voice from the sea, came a letter from the owners in New York. For some reason one of their vessels was without a captain. They understood that the man to whom they were writing had retired—but would he not make just one more trip to help them out? It was a summer voyage, a mere nothing, but it would be a great favor to them until they could make other arrangements, etc., etc.

Was the captain yearning for the sea after a year ashore? Would a vessel and sailors and the sound of wind in the rigging be welcome after months of his wife's talk and the tinkle of her piano, and visits among the neighbors, or sober work in the garden? Or, loath to go, did he feel the call of duty to his former employers?

We only know that he went to his wife and got her permission to retract his promise for this one voyage. Was it given unwillingly, I wonder, or was she reassured by the fact that this was to be a summer venture? At all events, she allowed her husband to go. The promise was to be in abeyance.

It is hardly necessary to end the story. If we were ancient Greeks we should say that Nemesis cares nothing for patchwork amendments. The oath had been given and broken. Summer voyage or not, the captain never returned, and all the bride's forebodings came true. Never again did the big square house hear its master's footsteps at the door; never again did he stride down the gravel walk to the summerhouse overlooking the harbor and the sea; he was not there to watch his son grow into manhood.

The Islands

ISLAND PEOPLE almost always develop very definite characteristics, occasionally bad but usually good. They are old-fashioned; the sea protects them from the flood of formlessness which washes across our towns and cities; they are franker, more individualistic; racier. Recently we were told a story of Monhegan, at a rather far remove, that illustrates the island quality.

An old woman died one early spring. There seemed to be no wood on hand suitable for a coffin. Not even an old dory. But in the fishhouse was a good topsail, a little too large, but useful enough once the reefs were tied.

At the funeral one little granddaughter marred the solemnity of the occasion by a sudden shout of laughter as Grandmother's body was lowered into the grave. Nothing was said at the time, but when the family were home again her mother turned to her:

"What did you mean, Almira, laughing like that when your grandmother was being buried?"

The little girl twisted her toe about on the rag rug.

"I know," she said, "it was awful. But I just couldn't help laughing when I thought of Grandma scudding to heaven in a close-reefed topsail!"

Lobstermen

IN THE DAYS when David the little bull roamed in peace down the lanes of Monhegan Island and the sheep throve unchidden on the short sweet grass above the Heads, a fisherman was drowned, as many have been—thrown overboard by some accident and carried quickly under by the weight of his great sea boots. As often happens the spot was not far from shore; and when the wind died down his widow had herself rowed out in a dory to the place where he had been last seen alive. She had several things on the dory seat, his family Bible, for instance, and his old pair of carpet slippers, and his cat, tied up in a sack, and held on her lap.

When the dory reached the spot of ocean which represented her husband's grave, the woman threw in her offerings, as simply as a widow of the Stone Age might have attempted to bring ease and comfort to the spirit of the dead. Then she had herself rowed back again and took up her life as best she could.

Mrs. Laura E. Richards told us the story, which went back to her girlhood summers on Monhegan a little before or perhaps a little after the Civil War. Now the fishing is done from motorboats, which go much farther and faster than the old lobster smacks or dories, but the hard life is the same. Several years ago, on a fine day at Westport Island, a lobsterman took out his little boy for a summer afternoon of hauling pots along the coves and inlets. The motorboat was found later, empty, going with the tide down to the sea; in another twenty-four hours the man's body was found, but never the child's. People shook their heads and sighed. Perhaps the little boy had grown cramped in the boat and asked to get out on a rock—one of those long dark-sided backs of stone which rise up out of the water with a matted fur of seaweed ever stirring about them. Safe as the rock may have looked in the sunshine, it would be easy to slip on the wet surface. Although a man could not swim, and had on his lobsterman's boots, a father would have gone in after his little son, willy-nilly. But only the sea gulls would have seen what actually happened.

The life is hard and dangerous, dangerous on a summer day, and more dangerous in winter. The lobster boats usually go out in pairs then, so that one may stand by the other in difficulties. Several winters ago two boats were hauling traps somewhere along the islands off Northeast Harbor. One of the men had some traps on a ledge above which the waves were apt to mount into high rollers, but without breaking.

On this particular day, while the other boat idled off the ledge, the first man went in to pull his traps. He had a boathook in one hand—a long wooden staff ending in a gaff and hook—with which he was hauling a buoy towards him, leaning well out over the gunwale while his boat tipped and tilted to the rollers.

Suddenly, against all expectation, a wave broke—broke over the boat and the leaning man, throwing him violently into the icy winter sea where his boots, after one floundering second, carried him feet-foremost straight down to the reef.

With incredible courage and coolness he held the boathook straight up over his head. His chance to stand so on the reef, the tip of his boathook visible in the hollow of the rollers, could last only a minute or two; and where one wave had broken, another might be expected to break, swamping another boat.

But his partner saw the gaff above the water, and in that split second ran his boat in beside it. Between breaker and breaker he got his grip on it while the man standing on the reef under the sea held on to the other end and was jerked and dragged back to safety and to life. Of all the lobstering stories I have heard on the coast, this seems to me the most remarkable, and the most creditable to the spirit of man.

On Monhegan

THE STORY OF MONHEGAN goes back into the mists of American history, to the early fishing boats and the fishermen who braved the Atlantic for cod, and dried their fish along the rocks of the islands and headlands, or on crude stages on the beaches. When the summer was over they sailed again for the ports of England or Brittany or the Basque coast. No chronicler ever voyaged with these men, little is known of their hardships or of their adventures. It was they who taught Samoset the English speech with which he greeted the Pilgrims at Plymouth; and from the fishermen came the smallpox which swept the Indian villages of the coast and often left whitening bones where the lodges had stood.

Monhegan was one of the most famous of the fishing stations; it was later an Indian trading station and several times served as a general refuge for the Maine settlers during Indian massacres. But the earliest gravestone we could find in the graveyard was late eighteenth century, to a little girl, Phoebe Starling. What a charming name!

There is another haunting name on the island. The large square gray house which looks down upon the narrow harbor has always been known as The Influence. It was built over a hundred years ago by one of the proprietors of the plantation, a Trefethren, and its calm tranquillity still dominates the village. Like so many old New England houses, it was left to two members of the builder's family; but the division—still maintained—was different from any other that I have ever seen. The widow had the entire front half of the house, overlooking the harbor and Manana; and the eldest son, the rear half, overlooking the lilacs and the gate leading to the twisting village road. There seems to be no tradition as to the quality of these people; only the house, with its quiet assurance and beauty, only the name are memorials to them.

We were sitting in a most charming room of a building beyond the village which stood close to the water, and had once been a fishhouse. I spoke of the drowned fisherman of whom we had been told, whose wife had thrown into the sea his Bible, his slippers, and his favorite cat, as a sort of offering, when his body was not found.

"Of course we remember," our hosts said. "This was his fishhouse, and he was drowned out of a dory right off here, between the shore and Nigh Duck Rock. But they *did* find his body, and they say he was standing upright, weighted down by his boots. He was the last of the Monhegan fishermen to wear the traditional bandanna and the gold loops in his ears, which were supposed to bring good luck."

One morning we woke to find that a west wind had driven away the fog, and that the mainland had appeared, bright and hard along nearly half the skyline. It was as though the island during the night had been towed in from the open sea and left anchored off the shore. Islands unseen before shared the blue of the ocean; Pemaquid Point was there, with the white of its surf and the lighthouse; the villages speckled the shore, and over them all rose the shadowy Camden Hills.

As we stood looking at them our companion remarked:

"I remember years ago once when I was on the Main I went back into the Camdens and they showed me a white cross high in the hills. They said that sometime in the 1850's a wedding party had gone there to gather flowers for the wedding which was to take place the next day. Everyone scattered, and the bride was last seen at the spot where the cross now stands. But she was never seen again and her body was never found. They call it still the Maiden's Chasm."

So, we had had to go to an island to learn that our familiar Camdens, seen in a thousand lights each day above the wooded ridges beyond our pond as we drive home to the farm from the Corners, have a ghost, the spirit of a bride, that white wraith which haunts the waterfalls of America, and stands upon many a Lover's Leap in our land.

I have since found more factual material about this same young girl in her crinolines and basque, with her hair no doubt drawn over her ears like two bird's-wings. They even say here on the mainland that her body *was* found. But I prefer the form that the instinct of folklore has given to the story. Now, when Henry and I rattle along the East Neck Road and my eye rests on the long outlines of the hills, I think of the lost bride who went out to gather flowers and was never seen again.

Three Men

"IT WAS one of those nights when you know things are wrong," Anna Glidden said. "The wind began blowing terribly from the southeast, and one of the maids and I got up and went about, closing and locking the windows to keep them from banging. You could feel the house shake, and it went on and on.

"In the morning I had the horses harnessed and drove over to Pemaquid Point. I knew there'd have been trouble there. And I was right. Two fishing boats had been lost, one after another, off the lighthouse. You know how the point runs out there, all rock and rockweed. Fifteen men had been drowned, and they had a row of bodies down in the boathouse, and my nephew went in to see them; but I didn't feel like it.

"There had been three men saved, who'd got up above the waves on the rock—an awful thing to have to do in the night with the breakers pounding on stone. I talked with one of the survivors. He was sunk. I don't think I ever saw a man more upset than he was. It seems that, as he was just getting his hands on some rockweed to try to make his landing on the next wave, he felt something come up near him, and a hand gripped his shoulder. He didn't know who it was. But the weight began tearing him loose from his hold on the weeds. He knew he didn't have any chance of getting out with the weight of two men, so he reached out and tore the hand off his shoulder. With the next wave he managed to get ashore, he didn't know how. But I tell you he was sunk, thinking about that hand and wondering which man it had belonged to.

"Of course anyone could understand how he felt. Listening to him, I felt badly myself. And next winter I happened to read that those three men had all been frozen to death in a gale off Cape Cod."

Island Kitchens

MISS BROWN raised her head and listened. Outside the open kitchen windows lay a small meadow where grew a few apple trees. Under one of these a couple of medium-sized lambs were tethered. Beyond the stone wall rose a further wall of spruces. It was a sunny day, but the blue of the sky was a little cooled by the remnants of fog. You could not see the water from the house, but you could hear it as a continual murmur along the rocky shores beyond the trees. You could hear the sea gulls and terns too, and a rooster crowing.

Olive Brown was not listening to any of these sounds, but to the whistle of some vessel coming into the island's small harbor.

"Sounds like the *Sunbeam,*" she remarked. "Didn't expect her this week. It's nearly time for the mail boat, but that isn't her whistle. The mail boat is running every day this summer. With so much mail and groceries coming in all the time, it makes it much harder for my brother down to the store."

We know the mission boat, nosing along the lonely coast, touching from island to island, holding services, taking off the sick, bringing doctors and work and counsel and talk of the outside world. A friend of ours went on several of its cruises one summer and told of a service of the Brethren of the Coast which she attended. An old man met them at the landing with a fiddle and played them up the path to the house where the service was to be held. A dozen or fifteen people were there, men, women, and children. They all sat about a kitchen table while the Bible was read, followed by a short talk, a prayer, and the singing of two or three hymns. Then they ate and drank together in a communion of shared dedication. That day it happened that the bread was pilot biscuit, and the wine was represented by ginger ale; but the devoutness which filled the room reminded our friend of primitive Christianity, and she said that the tears came to her eyes as she looked about the table at these island families partaking of the essential communion together.

The Brethren of the Coast do not form a sect, but merely a society suited to communities where perhaps in all truth only two or three may gather together with the bell buoys on the reefs to ring for their services. The members may belong to any church, but the churches cannot follow the lobster boats to these smaller rocky fragments of the coast; it is the *Sunbeam* which finds no weather too rough, no harborage too bleak for her visits, and brings hope to lonely communities and binds them together, so that even a single family on a bit of rock and spruce feels itself part of all the other life which clings to the islands and headlands, getting its existence from the sea.

The kitchen in which we sat, however, was a genial place. The stove was large and shining; dotted swiss curtains hung at the windows, and plants stood along the sills. This was a farm, and a prosperous one. The wool from its sheep, continually moistened by the fog, is softer and thicker than mainland wool. The blankets under which we slept at night were beautiful. They had been made from the farm's own wool at a little factory on the mainland, some blue, some rose, and some green.

Olive's father had just come back from the fair at Union.

"Did you go with him?" we asked.

She shook her head and hung up the dishcloths which she had just rinsed out.

"I never go to the Main if I can help it," she said. "I get so seasick always."

"But you were born on an island!" we cried, surprised.

"That doesn't keep me from being seasick," she answered stoutly. "Why, most of the women are—and a lot of the men, too. My uncle would never say he was going ashore until the morning of the day he left, so that he could be sure what kind of sea was running. No, we're many of us poor sailors, here."

She picked up a plateful of scraps to take out to the hens. "They like orts for a change."

Then she gave us a quick look.

"Do you know what orts are?"

We shook our heads, and she said: "I thought you wouldn't. Well, orts are scrapings from the dishes. Garbage is what has stood in the pail and turned sour."

An acquaintance came to take us calling, a small wrenlike woman who lived in a white house by the lily pond and hooked beautiful picture rugs. She had once made Henry a little rug of the Outermost House which he treasures.

On the road we passed a Ford with a young man and a girl in it. I say "passed," but actually *they* passed *us* several times, coming first from one direction and then from the other.

Miss Allerton smiled at them pityingly. "There's only a mile of road on the island," she explained, "but he's trying to give her a ride."

Her niece's kitchen was beyond any I have ever dreamed of. Olive Brown's kitchen was neat with a neatness which had an almost religious beauty and propriety, but this room fairly glittered. Everything which could shine, shone, and the rest glowed. The big stove looked as though it had just left the store. No, it was brighter and blacker than anything in a store, for hours upon hours of cleaning had given it the patina of devoted care.

The talk turned upon the church supper to be held at the end of the month.

"What are you going to bring?" asked Miss Allerton's niece.

Miss Allerton held her wrenlike head to one side and answered briskly:

"Nothing. The time has passed when I will cook for show. Cook for the hungry, I will; but for show, I will not. I'm not going to have my cake auctioned off again after the supper."

Her niece hastened to reassure her:

"But you know, Auntie, they just auction what happens to be

left at the end of the shelf."

Miss Allerton was neither convinced nor appeased.

"The world being what it is, Sarah, it always happens that what's at the end of the shelf is the worst of the food."

She turned the subject to other days on the island, to her brother and his lobstering. Old words live on in out-of-the-way places. They call the more rollicking hymns like "Throw Out the Life Line" (usually sung at midweek services), "pennyroyal hymns." They say that they are feeling "streaked," or so "waggy" that they can't keep themselves busy. They exclaim, "Want to know!" at a piece of news, or say that choppy water is "picketty." A busybody is a "fuddy-duddy." If you have stitches in your legs, you are "shanks-anxious." Instead of cleaning up, you "clem" up. The honesty by the door is still called "silver shillings," as the bright scarlet flower is called "redcoats." The fluff under the bed is known as "slut's wool"; good hay looks "stout"; straight ahead is "dead rabbit"; thunder at a distance is "white thunder," and heat lightning is "corn lightning." A light snow is "enough to track a cat"; you "flank" a sick person when you look after him; "glarmy" means clumsy; and "crud," annoyed.

These and a dozen other such words enliven speech, and give it an unexpectedness and a texture which make the simplest conversation interesting. And the things people say are delightful, like the old man's telling his niece that a setting hen's time wasn't worth a damn.

Much of Miss Allerton's life has been spent in cities. She has read many books and listened to concerts and lectures, but some of the old use of words clings to her tongue. When she told us how her brother had once carved his name and address on the claw of a lobster which he was sending to market, she said,

"He cut his hail on its claw, and within a week or two he had a letter from a man in New Haven. I don't know that he ever did it again, but that summer he got to wondering where his lobsters went to."

It was dusk as we walked home; the wind had changed, and

we could smell the sea strongly. Two jaegers were flying overhead with white marks like eyes staring down from their pointed wings. Far off we could see the blue outlines of the Camden Hills against the broken light of the sunset.

We found Olive Brown laying the table in the dining room. She asked about our call, and we mentioned the stove which had so impressed us.

"Yes," she agreed, "isn't it wonderful?" She hesitated, meaning to let her comment go at that; but after all she was human. She told the stove's secret. "When she has any real cooking to do, she does it on a stove they keep in the cellar. She uses the one in the kitchen just to boil water and such. No stove can look like that which ever has any frying done on it. I could have mine as shiny as hers, if I never used it."

Hermits

ANY HERMIT touches the imagination of the gregarious normal human being. We all have our hermit moments, and a man who goes to live by himself stirs our wonder and interest and a hidden sympathy in some part of our natures. I once met a pleasant German hermit at Palm Springs, California, in the old days before Hollywood discovered the spot. He lived by the stream in the cañon among the wild palms, and he had written little notices asking people not to kill rattlesnakes if they should come upon them: they were innocent creatures, seeking to harm no one. And in Arizona there was a peripatetic hermit with a great beard who came through the country once a year with a throng of dogs, some dogs pulling the cart in which the man sat, others following behind it fastened by cords, and two or three little dogs sitting with their master in the light wagon riding through deserts and across arid ranges.

I have been told, too, of a very disagreeable and suspicious hermit who used to live in the woods of New Hampshire. It is rather terrible to think of the sufferings of a timid hermit; and this man must have been very timid, for he had arranged a pit set with knives by his door, and had had scythes mortised into his chimney-mouth, as protection from intruders.

The hermit of Eagle Island was altogether different. I heard of him from a woman who as a child used to see him when her family visited the island for picnics. There had originally been two or three houses on the place, but the families had moved away, and only one old house and barn were left standing among the fields beyond the woods where the blue herons have their allegorical nests. At the other end of the island lay the small cliff-hung harbor where my friend's family moored their boat, in a narrow inlet.

During their first visits they were not aware that any other human being shared the island with them; but after a while they made out a figure watching them from behind a screen of trees. If they approached, the figure withdrew. The man had lived so long alone that he was desperately shy, but interested as a deer might be in the goings and comings of strangers. It was the mother of the family who suggested that they might leave out sandwiches, a cup of coffee, and a banana when they went for their stroll about the heronry; and when they came back the food was gone. Bit by bit, they gained the hermit's confidence. Slowly he showed himself more openly; at last came the day when he would sit with them, although still with an air of arrested flight. They learned that he owned the island now and lived here winter and summer without so much as a cat or dog to share his solitude. He caught fish and, for the rest, drank a gruel of cornmeal stirred in water. On this Spartan diet he had lived for years.

In due course of time the picnickers bought the island. I asked what the hermit did then, expecting to hear that he had gone on living in the gray house to which he was accustomed. But no, by no means! he used the money to go to New Bedford, and there he worked as a sailmaker, accustoming himself once more to human ways.

"And, oh, yes," my friend added, "he was very fond of reading books and magazines, particularly the *Atlantic*. Father used to send him his copy every month."

Old Men

HERE in the country districts many widowers hire housekeepers to cook for them and do the chores proper to a woman. But our neighbor, Mr. Ricker's father (or was it his grandfather?), lived on alone in the gray low house which is now empty. When people asked him why he didn't marry So-and-so, he would shake his head and always give the same answer: "I don't want any old geranium."

But he was undoubtedly lonely, and very often would appear at a kitchen door in the afternoon with his lantern in hand. The woman of the place would give one glance at the lantern, and plan on a larger supper. Everyone here is kind and hospitable. It would be with real warmth that he was invited to sit down with them.

"No," he would answer politely. "I've had supper." But the neighbors would press the point and he would yield at last.

"Fact's the case [his phrase for every occasion], I will, just to be sociable."

After supper, he would sit talking in the kitchen until he fell asleep in his chair. Then someone would light the lantern beside him and put it back, and the people of the house would tiptoe out, lamp in hand, and go to bed, leaving the old man asleep by the stove. They did not wish to rouse him and perhaps embarrass him by telling him that it was time for them to be abed, with a day's haying before them. No, with the natural delicacy and good manners which one finds everywhere here, they left the old man to his sleep. Sometime during the night he would wake up and take his waiting lantern and go home to his lonely house along the lonely road.

Our Lawrence was telling us the other day of another old man who used to come every year to his father's farm selling seeds. He must have been nearly eighty years old, but when the spring came and the frost had gone out of the ground he would drive up to the door with his seed corn and barley, his melon seeds, beans, peas, lettuce, and cabbages. He probably had flower seeds as well, for the women usually like to have a garden by the back steps. When the trading was over he was always invited to dinner, and came in and ate heartily.

On the surface there is nothing strange about that; but, having known the old man for years, the neighbors also knew that he stopped at half a dozen farms in a row and had a hearty dinner at each. They would compare notes afterward and then exclaim in admiration, "Lord, where does he *put* it all?" for he was a withered cricket of an old man. And next year when his buggy wheels sounded once more along the road and stopped at the mailbox and he hoisted himself out between the wheels, they were eager to invite him in to dinner again and to marvel once more at his remarkable prowess as an eater.

Sometimes more surprising things may happen. A few years ago there was an old man living on what had once been a very fine farm about five miles out of town. The house was large although badly in need of paint, and the barn had been built to hold a dozen cows and a team of horses. A good shed with an open veranda ran between the two.

The old man, who had been a widower for twenty years, had moved permanently into the kitchen. Winter and summer, indoors and out, he wore a moth-eaten coonskin cap; and for a bed he used a dresser which he kept close to the stove. A strange thing was the piano which stood against one wall with a hymn book on it open at the hymn which had been played for Lincoln's funeral. He could not play the piano himself; but now and then, when people came to see him, he asked them to play the hymn for him, and they would pick their way across the littered floor, pull out the dusty piano stool, and play it to please him.

As the years went by, more and more windows were boarded

up, and the garden patch grew smaller. He sold all his stock and farm machinery, and most of the furniture in the big echoing shell of a house. A nephew in New Jersey was said to be willing to have him board with him, but no one could see where he was to get the money unless he could sell the farm, and that had had a For Sale sign nailed to the elm by the gate nearly as long as people could remember. It is true that the buildings had a fairly large insurance on them, placed in better days, which he had somehow managed to keep paid up. But what good did that do him?

At last one fall the old man left the house and locked the door behind him on its empty rooms, and the untidy kitchen with the mattress and quilts still thrown over the dresser and the piano against the wall. He was to stay with distant relatives in town, and later he was to go to his nephew's, although no one understood the details of the arrangements.

One night about a week after he had left, after a cold lowering day, someone on a neighboring farm awakened and noticed a curious light coming in at his windows and, looking out, saw that the empty farmhouse was on fire. All the neighbors went over, but there was not much that they could do. Snow was falling and the ground, which had been bare that afternoon, was already white. The fire was too far advanced to be checked by such pails of water as they might be able to pull up one by one from the old well. There was not so much as a cat to be saved; and no one intended to risk his skin for the deserted dresser, the out-of-tune piano, or the kitchen chairs.

The men and one or two of their wives stood about in a little group watching the splendor of the fire as the old place turned into smoke and ashes before their eyes, with that interest in catastrophes, that hypnotized attention which a large fire naturally awakens.

"Might have been tramps," one man said after a while.

"Might have been," agreed another.

In the town the news did not arrive until morning, and the

old man received word of it somewhat stolidly over doughnuts and coffee at the kitchen table. He had been in bed on the third floor since eight-thirty the night before, as everyone in the house knew. Of course he had been out all that afternoon. There was nothing unusual about that. Every day he did an errand or two and walked out a little along the highway. If a passing motorist had picked up an old man thumbing a ride, if someone had taken the lane through the woods in from the highway, if a candle in a basket in the cellar had burned slowly to the paper and rags at its base, no one was the wiser. Who can say what may have happened?

And the snow had covered any possible footprint of an intruder, whether of tramp or of someone accustomed to those narrow paths through the long grass.

The neighbors were glad when the insurance was paid and the old man had a little money in the bank for his last days. They saw him off warmly as he took the train for New Jersey and his nephew's house.

"Always a great one to foretell the weather," one man remarked reflectively.

"He could smell a storm coming as good as a cat," said another.

The American Tradition

TODAY the sea fog lies close-pressed to our hayfields, so that we cannot see the lake nor the wooded heights to the west which once were pasture land and now are growing up again to pine. Even the big maples over the farm graveyard are as though they were not. Only the nearer barn, the martin house on its pole, and an old apple stump which should have been cut down long ago show dimly through the cloud in which we lie.

Here at the kitchen table, looking into the open fire, listening to its flowing sound broken only occasionally by a faint snap, I am aware that in regard to time we live always in a white vapor, seeing only a little of what lies about us, knowing only a few of the nearer landmarks.

A man's life or a woman's after a hundred years is usually summed up by little more than an old daguerreotype, a few letters stiffly written, breaking along the folds, or the mute witness of the objects they perhaps cherished: "These were my grandmother's earrings. This was my great-grandfather's desk." Yet perhaps the grandmother never cared for the earrings; perhaps the great-grandfather preferred to write at a table (as I am writing now) in the kitchen. We can never tell. These things were theirs: we know that at least. And a few stories have come down to us, having escaped shipwreck on the shoals of the indifference of each new generation. More solid still is the work of their hands, the blankets which the women wove, the houses and barns and walls that the men built. Yet who did what?

Usually the work has been worn anonymous by time; the stories have become fables: "Long ago, when I was young, there was a man . . ." So the individual is lost, or almost lost; but out of the accumulation of tales remembered, out of the quality of the village houses, the barns with their beamwork sometimes as fine as in a church, the laborious walls, the vessels built in the coves, comes a sense of the entire people, vague, often contradictory, but still real.

To most of us a wilderness is not very interesting. Human life must have been lived in a place, and have developed its especial pattern, its achievements and failures. There must be some dignity of the spirit to make earth and forest and river alive to us and part of us. Compared to that of most countries, our native folklore is thin; it has had only a little over three hundred years in which to accumulate.

Behind it lies the culture of the Indians, seen by us almost entirely in two dimensions. Except to a few archaeologists, Indian history began with the arrival of the first white explorers and exists no further back than in white records. In the Indian past, a thousand years is as a day. And yet that day was strange and colorful, with something of the beauty, mystery, and cruelty of nature. We see our own history against the backdrop of forests and mountains and of a people almost as native as they. The Indian has always interested us: his image has lain across our imagination like the shadow of a pine across a meadow. Our American tradition is comparatively young; but it has its own tart flavor, its dignities, its poignancies, and its sudden contrasts. The sun is bright above it, the frost heaves the ground on which it stands, the northwest wind blows over it. It is not to be belittled.

So I have gathered together these stories which were all told me by neighbors. Some of the tales may have strayed from truth and been shaped into folklore. A man only last night assured me that his old guide on Katahdin told him that the caribou moved away of their own accord north into Canada, swimming, I suppose, the wide St. Lawrence, disappearing towards the Arctic. But a friend earlier told me of the sumaclike branched horns of the caribou which he had seen at the bottom of the Katahdin cliffs. So with all these stories: I cannot vouch for them. I can only say that I heard them with my own ears, some once, some many times, and wrote them down as I heard them, because it seemed to me that a bringing-together of many stories from one focus has a certain value in giving the emotional background of a locality.

And if Americans are to become really at home in America it must be through the devotion of many people to many small, deeply loved places. The field by the sea, the single mountain peak seen from a man's door, the island of trees and farm buildings in the western wheat, must be sung and painted and praised until each takes on the gentleness of the thing long loved, and becomes an unconscious part of us and we of it. For we are not yet at ease with our land, and it is restive and often sullen with us, like a horse which has been roughly broken to riding, and is left frequently standing uncared for in the sleet.